EXPLORING THE KETTLE VALLEY RAILWAY

Exploring the Kettle Valley Railway

Beth Hill

POLESTAR
BOOK PUBLISHERS

EXPLORING THE KETTLE VALLEY RAILWAY
Copyright © 1989 by Beth Hill

Published by

Polestar Press Ltd., R.R. 1, Winlaw, B.C., V0G 2J0, 604-226-7670

Canadian Cataloguing in Publication Data
Hill, Beth, 1924 —
Exploring the Kettle Valley Railway
Includes bibliographical references.
ISBN 0-919591-44-2
1. Kettle Valley Region (B.C.) - Description and travel - Guide-books.
2. Kettle Valley Railway - History.   3. Railroads - British Columbia -
Kettle Valley Region - History. I. Title.
FC 384.5K57A3 1989   917.11'41   C89-091625-X
F1089.K57H5 1989

Acknowledgements
Thanks to the B.C. Archives and Records Service, the pub-
lisher of the *Sound Heritage Series*, for permission to quote from
SHS No. 31 (*Railroads*, written by Robert Turner); and to Clare
McCallister for her lively comments. The poem, ''The Kettle
Valley Ghost Train,'' was first printed in the 51st Report of
the Okanagan Historical Society, and is here reprinted through
the kindness of the author, Arnold Jones.

Cover design by Jim Brennan
Cover photographs by Murphy Shewchuk
Interior illustrations by Tim Williamson

Table of Contents

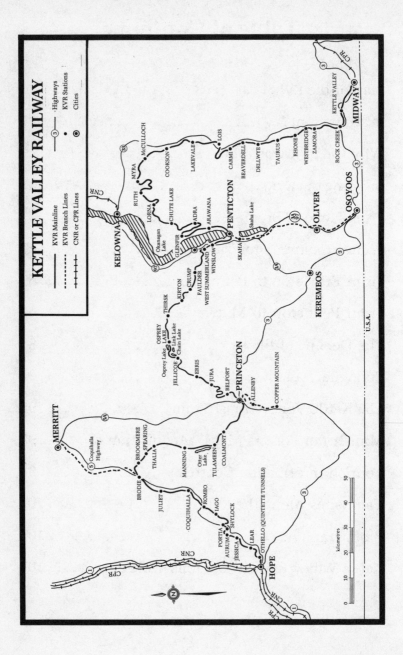

KETTLE VALLEY RAILWAY

— KVR Mainline
- - - KVR Branch Lines
+++ CNR or CPR Lines

③ Highways
• KVR Stations
◎ Cities

Introduction

Perhaps this spunky little railroad should never have been built. Blasted, battered and tunnelled over and through three mountain ranges, its costs were as high as the ridges it crossed, and when it was completed there were crushing snowfalls, avalanches, landslides and forest fires to contend with. The men of the Kettle Valley Railway continually repelled Nature's attacks, but they could do nothing about the building of the Hope-Princeton Highway, and the competition from cars and trucks which ultimately caused the KVR's decline and death. When its demise was imminent, thousands of British Columbians rallied to try and staunch its ebbing life. They understood the enemies of the Kettle Valley Railway — the bitter winters, the drenching rains and landslides, the unprofitable economics, the perils of a precipitous terrain combined with long uninhabitable distances—but they grieved when its owners, the Canadian Pacific Railway Company, shut it down.

Now, although the steel is gone (except on the Penticton to Brookmere section), the roadbed loops across southern British Columbia and many of the tunnels and spectacular trestles are still intact. At times the roadbed is inconspicuous as you often cannot see more than a few metres of it at a time and also because, for the most part, it is disguised as a path or gravel road. But it is there and it is accessible from many places. That is the purpose of this guide: to help people find the old "KV" and to encourage them to join the growing numbers of Kettle Valley Railway buffs. If there are enough of us, perhaps we can save the line as a 500 kilometre hiking and biking trail. It is logical to make use of an existing corridor for non-motorized traffic. Once broken up, such a route as this could never again be assembled. The growing interest in recreation and the need for natural tourist attractions make the development of a Kettle Valley Railway hiking and biking trail an economically feasible project, for it would become a world-renowned resource. This was a railway like none other.

Moreover, we should preserve the astounding Myra Canyon as a monument to the railroad men who constructed the railroads through this craggy land and who kept the Kettle Valley Railway running from 1916 to 1962.

If Canada has a national colour, it is not the red of Eastern maple leaves or the red of the Mounted Police. It's CPR red, the tuscan red of the railway that united this almost empty land. The faint sound of a mournful steam whistle haunts our memories. When you are walking along the abandoned right of way and the wind shivers the golden aspen, you can almost hear that whistle around the next bend....

Why the Kettle Valley Railway Was Built

To lure British Columbia into the Canadian confederation in 1867, the Canadian Pacific Railway to the Pacific was promised—a ribbon of steel that would bind the Dominion from the Atlantic to Pacific. Laying tracks across the prairies was easy, but the high north-south ranges of the coast mountains were a challenge indeed. They chose the easiest route, swinging north through

Banff then south down the Fraser to Vancouver. But this completely isolated the Kootenay region in south-eastern British Columbia. In 1885 the CPR's last spike was driven at Craigellachie. With bunting and beer and marching bands this fledgling nation celebrated the completion of the longest railway in the world; but the Kootenays were left out.

Two years after the last spike, when the cheering had died away, two Americans, the Hall brothers, brought a sackful of incredibly rich Kootenay silver ore into Butte, Montana. This started a stampede of Americans into the isolated southeastern corner of B.C. American miners swarmed north by the thousands. All the country between Greenwood and Grand Forks was soon staked with mining claims. In those heady days, Greenwood had twenty-nine saloons. The wealth seemed limitless, but instead of flowing into Canadian hands, it was all being siphoned off southwards to the United States, enriching (among others) a strong-willed railway tycoon named James Jerome Hill. British Columbian businessmen in Vancouver and Victoria, watching the wealth departing on American railways, became angry and bitter. The need for a railway from the Kootenays to the coast became a political issue which elected or defeated successive provincial governments.

James Jerome Hill (Canadian by birth), the greatest of the railway empire builders, had a terrible temper. He has been described as "the barbed-wire, shaggy-headed, one-eyed old son of a bitch of Western railroading." To push his Great Northern Railroad across the continent he waged war with everyone and everything. Hill had once been a director of the CPR, but after stormy battles with CPR president William Van Horne (an American by birth), Hill resigned, swearing "I'll get even with him if I have to go to hell for it and shovel coal!" Now, Hill's Great Northern

Railroad had spurs running north to suck Canada's wealth. Van Horne was determined that the CPR would "Mop the floor with the Great Northern or any other American company extending its lines into the Northwest."

The battle between the two railway giants was fought with a rash of railways, in the twenty-five years from 1893 on. When J. J. Hill and Van Horne grew old, the battle was carried on by J.J.'s son Louis and Thomas Shaughnessy of the CPR. The Kettle Valley Railway was the CPR's last card, but it won the game for Canada.

Some of the railways built during that time included the SF&N (Spokane Falls & Northern Railway, 1889); GN (Great Northern Railway, J.J. Hill); C & K (Columbia & Kootenay Railway and Transportation Co., 1891); N & FS (Nelson & Fort Shepherd Railway, 1893); K & S (Kaslo & Slocan Railway, 1893, bought by Hill in 1894); C & W (Columbia & Western Railway, H.A. Heinze, 1896); N & S (Nakusp & Slocan Railway, CPR); VV & E (Vancouver, Victoria & Eastern Railway, 1896); KVRR (Kettle Valley River Railway, 1901); M & V (Midway & Vernon Railway, 1901, but never built); W & GN (Washington & Great Northern Railway, 1901, J. J. Hill); and the NK & S (Nicola, Kamloops & Similkameen Railway, 1905, CPR).

The rest of this chapter tells how the two giants, the CPR and the GN, fought to control rail transport out of the Kootenays. Those eager to get on the road may skip some of the details, while others, wanting to know even more, should select from the books listed in the bibliography at the back of this book.

The first railway into the Kootenays, built in 1889 (two years after the Hall Brothers' silver strike), was the Spokane Falls and Northern Railway, constructed by Daniel Corbin, from Spokane to Colville (just south of the United States border). It was soon extended into British Columbia. This railway was later purchased by J.J. Hill's American

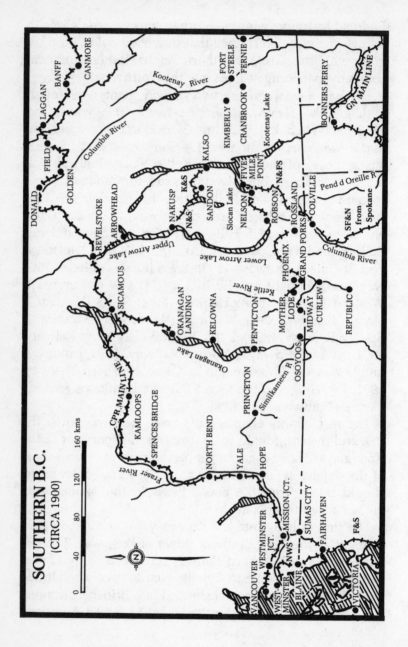

SOUTHERN B.C.
(CIRCA 1900)

railway company, the Great Northern. Dismayed by the intrusion of the American railway, in 1891 the CPR fought back by building the Columbia & Kootenay Railway, a portage railway between Robson and Nelson. This enabled the CPR to take out the silver ore from Nelson on steam vessels to the CPR mainline at Revelstoke at the north end of the Arrow Lakes. Two years later, in 1893, American money built the Nelson & Fort Shepherd Railway, to join Nelson to the Spokane Falls and Northern Railway. Again, this enabled rich Kootenay ore to be carried south to the United States.

In 1896, F. August Heinze, an American, petitioned the British Columbian government for permission to build the Columbia and Western Railway, to carry the concentrate from his smelter at Trail Creek (on the Columbia River, just below Rossland) to Penticton, where his railway would connect with the CPR boats on Lake Okanagan. This railway would give Heinze an independent outlet, so that neither the CPR nor Corbin's SF & N could break his lucrative Rossland monopoly. The activities of Heinze, Hill and Corbin pressured Van Horne to get a CPR line into the Kootenays. When the Liberal government of Sir Wilfred Laurier indicated its willingness to share costs, the surveying of the Crowsnest Pass began in the winter of 1896, even before negotiations with the government were concluded. Anticipating federal funds, Van Horne had already ordered the steel. Unpaid bills were piling up. Determined to begin construction in the spring, Van Horne needed money. He suggested to Laurier that the railway might consider a rate reduction throughout the entire west if a substantial cash grant were immediately forthcoming. Anticipating many votes from the grateful Western farmers, the Ottawa machinery began to roll like a runaway freight train. Van Horne got the cash ($11,000 per mile, up to a total of $3,630,000), and in exchange, promised to reduce freight rates on some commodities, notably grain. As Canadians know, this Crowsnest Agreement of 1897 is still a controversial issue.

So the CPR line into the Kootenays went full steam ahead, and the Lethbridge to Kootenay Lake section was finished in 1898. That same year the CPR purchased Heinze's still-unfinished Columbia and Western Railway. In 1900, the first CPR train rolled into Midway. Now the CPR had access to the area from the east, but there was still no connection between the Kootenays and the western coast.

In 1901, J. J. Hill, making the first move in a new GN offensive against the CPR, acquired control of the proposed Vancouver, Victoria and Eastern Railway. This, according to railway historian Barrie Sanford, "gave him carte blanche to economically rape the Boundary area." The VV & E, first promoted by British Columbian businessmen in 1896, had a charter for the Kootenay-Coast connection. J. J. Hill had bought control of Corbin's SF & N in 1898, running from Spokane to Colville, and now the purchase of the VV & E gave him the hope of achieving his life's desire: a railway line from Chicago to Vancouver.

The year 1901 also saw the birth of the Midway and Vernon Railway, promoted by a group of Greenwood citizens. It was granted a charter and a $4000 per mile subsidy and was to follow the Kettle River northward, crossing a relatively low ridge to reach Vernon. Vernon was also the end of the Shuswap and Okanagan Railway, a CPR subsidiary built in the 1890s. Thus the Midway and Vernon gained an indirect rail link both to Vancouver and the East. When its owners had difficulty raising the necessary capital, the M & V was called the Makeshift and Visionary Railway. The subsidy was raised to $5000 per mile but still no financier was interested. By 1906 the M & V was dead. However, this "paper railway" was destined to be another piece of the KVR.

Also in 1901 a Canadian group, led by Tracy Holland, got a charter for a railway called the Kettle River Valley Railway, to connect the mine at Republic (30 miles south of the border) with the Granby smelter at Grand Forks. Like mice challenging a cat, they stood in the way of J. J. Hill's plans for the Washington and Great Northern Railway. The little company put up a good fight, but by 1907 Hill had all but destroyed it. The track laid to Republic was soon overgrown with weeds. Hill's Washington and Great Northern ran along the Kettle River Valley to Grand Forks, looped south into the U.S. to Curlew, and then turned north to re-enter Canada at Midway. From there it went through Rock Creek and back into American territory to Oroville.

In 1905 Hill won an important victory when the Laurier government passed a bill amending the VV & E charter to allow part of the line to go through the United States. The bitter rivalry between Hill and the CPR broke into a mini war in September, 1905. In the battle of Midway, more than three hundred CPR men, armed with shovels and picks, marched across the Kettle Valley and attacked the VV & E men building line on a disputed piece of land. The valley was noisy with the clang of shovels, angry shouting and revolver shots fired into the air, and when darkness fell there were many bruises and a few broken limbs. Police intervened and the battle was transferred to the courts. Although the judge called Hill "highhanded", the VV & E was finally granted the correct expropriation order, and the rivals returned to fighting with railroads instead of shovels.

In 1907 Louis Hill had succeeded his father as president, but the old man kept his hand on the throttle. In 1908 the VV & E was extended from Oroville, Washington, to Keremeos. In 1909, the steel was laid through to Hedley and Princeton. (In 1948, Highway 3, following the old Dewdney Trail route along the north side of the Similkameen River, was built over this GN roadbed.) In gratitude to Hill, the Princeton citizens renamed the Similkameen River the Jimhillameen. Hill had just announced that his railroad would go through the Hope Mountains with an eight mile tunnel, the longest railway tunnel in North America. He immediately planned to extend the VV & E from Princeton up the Kettle River to Tulameen. With his VV & E across the Hope Mountains, Hill would at last have won the battle with the CPR for the southern British Columbia trade.

However, the CPR was also laying steel. In 1907 the CPR had opened the Nicola, Kamloops & Similkameen Railway, from Spences Bridge on the Fraser River through Merritt to Nicola, to gain access to the Nicola Valley's exposed seams of bituminous coal. Expecting that Nicola would become the divisional point on an extension to Midway, Joseph Guichon built a plush hotel at Quilchena, (which still serves fine meals to tourists and local ranching families). But when the extension was built, it went southward from Merritt up the Coldwater Valley, not east from Nicola via Quilchena Creek. As a result of that decision, Nicola remains much as it was almost a century ago while Merritt boomed into a small city.

Many miles of rugged mountains still separated the end of the CPR line at Midway from the coast. In 1908, James John Warren, an Ontario lawyer who had taken over the financial problems of the almost defunct Kettle River Valley Railway, arranged to sail across the Atlantic on the Empress of Britain. He knew one of the passengers would be Thomas G. Shaughnessy, Van Horne's successor as president of the CPR. Warren wanted Canadian control of the transportation link with the coast and he wanted to unload the unprofitable KRVR. Shaughnessy, in contrast to

his enemy J.J. Hill, who rarely visited Canada, deeply loved British Columbia. He had even founded other businesses there, including the Summerland Development Company which made Okanagan fruit world famous. On board the Atlantic liner, Warren and Shaughnessy discussed maintaining Canadian control of the Kootenay wealth and the extension of the CPR west of Midway. Shaughnessy then met B.C.'s Premier McBride who agreed to support the CPR scheme. First he called an election on the issue and won an overwhelming vote of confidence from British Columbians. The terms of agreement were that the KVR would acquire the assets and debts of the Midway and Vernon Railway; the KVR would complete the Midway to Nicola line within four years; the government would give a subsidy of $5,000 per mile for the line between Penticton and the Nicola line; the KVR would have free right-of-way through crown lands; and the KVR would have a temporary exemption from some taxes.

One crucial section was not discussed. The Coquihalla extension, which had been omitted from the agreement, was to become the site of the last battle between the GN and the CPR. Leaving Premier McBride, Shaughnessy then went to Ottawa to present the proposition to the unenthusiastic CPR directors. He gained their assent, but their forebodings about the terrain and the climate were well founded. As a result of these talks, in 1910 Warren became president of the renamed Kettle Valley Railway, now a CPR subsidiary. That same year construction was started at both Merritt and Midway to build a railway which would connect Midway to the main CPR line at Spences Bridge.

Andrew McCullough was hired as chief engineer. This remarkable engineer deserves more recognition than he has received. Born to a poor farming family in Ontario in 1864, his only formal training was as an accountant. When his family could do without his labour, he came west to work in a lumber mill near Seattle. These were hard times and he was glad to get what work he could. A keen reader and always eager to learn, McCullough would row across Puget Sound to attend Shakespearean performances in a Seattle theatre, then row back through the night to be at work the next day. As he rowed with a steady stroke, his eye on the shore lights for guidance, the Shakespearian actors would strut once more on the stage of his imagination, their lines echoing in his mind. The names of some of the KVR stations, such as Juliet and Iago, reflect these memorable evenings. At age thirty he got a job with the CPR, repairing their mainline after the spring flooding, then worked with a bridge gang along the Thompson River. He then took a railway job in Michigan where he gained the status of resident engineer. Returning to B.C., he worked on the Nakusp and Slocan branch line before he was asked to do a survey of the CPR Crow's Nest line. Rapidly promoted to Assistant Engineer and then to Division Engineer, in 1910, at age 46, he was recognized by Shaughnessy as the engineer to undertake this most difficult and expensive of all railroad projects. When McCulloch and Warren met, they formed a deep and enduring friendship. Acknowledging their integrity and intelligence, Shaughnessy gave them only one order: the KVR must be first class in every way.

In 1912 it was clear that the end of the war between the Canadian and American railroads would be fought in the Coquihalla Valley. The route of the VV & E, northwards up the Tulameen Valley, skipped from one side of the river to the other, effectively excluding a second railroad. Construction on the proposed tunnel through the Hope Mountains and emerging into the Coquihalla Valley had been started in 1910. However, such a long tunnel would

take years to blast, and the KVR, coming from the other direction, could win the race for the Coquihalla where there was only room for one railway. This was the winning card in the thirty-year-old game, the key to hauling the mineral wealth from the Kootenays. However, before adopting the tunnel route, the VV & E had surveyed and filed a route proposal through the Coquihalla Canyon. Consequently, when the KVR crews arrived to begin work in the pass, Hill was waiting for them with an injunction. In 1912, the Board of Railway Commissioners recommended that the Chief Engineers of each railroad should get together to plan a double-track route. In the 1912 election, Premier McBride was re-elected on a platform of further financial support for the KVR ($10,000 per mile through Coquihalla Pass plus $200,000 for a combined car and railroad bridge across the Fraser at Hope) while offering nothing to the VV & E. When McBride gained a landslide victory, it was plain that Canadians wanted a Canadian railway.

In November 1912, the KVR announced that it would build the line from the Loop near Brookmere to the Coquihalla summit and would give the VV & E running rights. In exchange, the VV & E would give the KVR running rights over the eight miles from Brookmere to Thalia. But this agreement, amazingly cooperative as it was, did not solve the major point of dispute—the Coquihalla Pass. Further talks took place between the competing railroads and in April, 1913, the war was over. A single line would be shared by both corporations. "Railways Bury Hatchet" announced the *Similkameen Star* on April 18, 1913. The KVR would build and own the 54 miles from Brookmere to Hope and the GN, on behalf of the VV & E, would have trackage rights in exchange for an annual fee. The KVR gained the use of the line down the Tulameen Valley. The agreement was almost a GN surrender.

What had happened? Circumstances had changed since the early days of the fight between the American GN and the Canadian CPR. Increased government regulation of railways and the rising power of railway unions were factors leading to a policy of peaceful co-existence of railways on the continent. The imminent war in Europe was a sobering influence on everyone. The depression in the economy which preceded this war limited the expansion capital available to the railways. And the expense of the proposed GN tunnel and Coquihalla Pass construction were more than the GN was willing to invest. But, above all, J. J. Hill had counted on a free trade agreement between the U.S. and Canada, opening Canadian resources to American exploitation. Prime Minister Laurier had campaigned on this issue in 1911, but Canadians, fearing U.S. power, had defeated Laurier. This ended J. J. Hill's dream of free trade carried, very profitably, on his railroads. J. J. Hill died on May 29, 1916, just two months before the railway through the Coquihalla Pass was opened. As a token tribute to him, Louis Hill and a group of GN officials rode over the line from Vancouver to Spokane via Princeton on September 27 and 28, 1916, on board a special Great Northern train, technically fulfilling Hill's dream. This was the only GN train ever to run through the Coquihalla Pass.

So the Canadians won their railroad and the astounding Kettle Valley Railroad was built.

Building the Kettle Valley Railway

Black powder and muscle power built the Kettle Valley Railway. Construction began in 1910, but business was booming in Canadian railway building and, consequently, skilled workers were scarce. McCullough got no replies to his ads and gloomily threatened to build the road himself. Even unskilled jobs were not filled in spite of a good pay rate—two dollars per day. Because of the labour shortage, progress was slow during the first years; after two years only 20 per cent had been built. However, in 1912 the Canadian government removed restrictions on workers from other countries and by the end of that year nearly 5,000 men were at work on the KVR, speaking a babel languages. Then, in 1914, thousands of railway workers went to war and progress on the KVR slowed down again.

With as many as five boxcar loads of explosives used in a single blast, a phenomenal amount of black powder was required. When the dust of the blast had settled, the labourers moved in with picks and shovels and a few horse-drawn scrapers to clear the rubble. (Not until 1951, almost the end of the KVR era, were bulldozers introduced, the same year that the first diesel engines were purchased.) The rock on the Penticton to Hydraulic Lake section was so hard that black powder wasn't powerful enough; fortunately a new explosive, 90 per cent nitroglycerine, was developed in 1913. But there were many accidents with explosives, usually because of careless handling. Nitroglycerine froze in below-zero temperatures; sometimes when the workmen were unwilling to wait for the slow thawing in hot water, they would place the dynamite near an open fire. Some even roasted it in a frying pan.

"I've been workin' on the railroad, all the live-long day" — this is a song that everyone used to sing, but today few remember the harsh reality—the long, hard, backbreaking work with shovel and pick, the processions of teams of horses or mules dragging scrapers, the hard-rock miners blasting out the rock cuts, the little muck cars pulled and pushed by manpower to move the breakaway. When the grade was built, the track-laying machine arrived. Arthur Stiffe, who as a fourteen-year-old worked as a water-boy with a track-laying gang, has described the rail gangs of between 65 and 85 men living twelve to a car in bunk cars. Behind the big track layer were about six cars packed with rails and ties all stacked up, that had conveyor belts on the side for bringing the rail or ties to the front. Behind the rail and tie cars were cars carrying spikes, bolts, and pickaroons. The foreman would be up ahead about 50 feet with a sight-board, and when the rail was properly placed on the ties, five men on each side would pound in the huge spikes to hold the rails in place. The track-layer then

moved forward on the new rails. "It is surprising how much rail you can lay. In one day we laid 2 1/4 miles of track," he said. Once the ties and rail had been laid, the crews return to ballast, to keep the tracks aligned and well-drained. They jacked up the track and shovelled gravel under the ties to keep the tracks elevated. Another crew followed to fill in under and around each tie.

Construction costs were high and were never recovered by the CPR. Although the KVR made an operations profit by carrying ore, coal, lumber, fruit, passengers, mail and general freight, the construction debt—about $20 million in 1916—was never repaid.

In the winter the crews fought the cold and the snow and in the summer the intense heat created another danger—forest fires. In 1931 a fire near Portia threatened to burn out a dozen railway bridges. When this fire was brought under control, another one started near Juliet and headed towards Brookmere. Expecting Brookmere to be destroyed, the railway got a dozen boxcars onto the track to evacuate the residents, but a sudden change in wind direction saved the station. Another fire that year did a great deal of damage to the line near Carmi, and only a week later a huge fire threatened the spectacular trestles of Myra Canyon. Tank cars loaded with water were sent to the site and the crews choked in the thick smoke as they struggled to keep the trestles wet.

It was a dangerous railroad. One of the worst accidents occurred on Labour Day in 1926, a day adorned with shimmering aspens, and thin veils of mist drifting in the Coquihalla Valley. The engineer, Bob Marks, and Ray Letts, the fireman, climbed on board locomotive 3401 for a routine run to Hope. There were eighteen cars in tow—ore cars carrying lead and zinc ingots from Trail, a few flat cars with automobiles, and a caboose, plus a pusher to help them get their heavy load up the grade to

Coquihalla. On this run the pusher locomotive was going through to Hope to help bring up a train scheduled to go east that afternoon. On the uphill grade from Brodie to the Coquihalla summit, the sweaty fireman Ray Letts shovelled coal.

At Coquihalla twelve cars of coal, left by a freight turning at Coquihalla the night before, were added to the train. Brakes were tested for the long downhill run to Hope. Engineer Bob Marks noticed that a few boys, fruit-pickers from the Okanagan, had jumped the train for a

free ride back to Vancouver. The train left Coquihalla and stopped at Iago for the required time to cool the wheels. After leaving Iago, the train began to accelerate. Marks reached for the brake lever. There was a hiss, then total silence. No more air. Marks instantly whistled the signal for the crew to man the hand brakes. If enough hand brakes could be set immediately, perhaps the train could be stopped. But the grade was too steep and the train was already moving too fast. Young Bob Barwick managed to crawl out on the catwalk of the swaying helper engine as the train rocketted down the rails. He heroically succeeded in freeing it from the rest of the train, so that he could brake his half of the train. Bringing his section under control, Barwick had to watch as the runaway disappeared around a curve ahead, with every crew member on top of the train, manning the hand brakes. The runaway train thundered through Jessica with flames leaping from the brakeshoes. Three coal cars and the caboose broke off and crashed into the Jessica water tower. The section foreman at Jessica heard the horrible crash when the runaway flew into the canyon. Then—silence.

The locomotive and twenty-five freight cars burned and four men died in the wreck. The number of boys was not known, so the inquest set the death toll at eleven. Since all evidence had been destroyed, the cause of the accident could not be determined. Despite a number of accidents, the KVR had the best safety record on the continent and it was said that no passengers were ever killed; apparently the young fruit-pickers didn't count.

Part of the explanation for the KVR safety record was McCullough's supervision. In the first years of construction he was constantly on horseback, checking the quality of the work. After the KVR was in operation, track cars, or in winter a plow train, often went ahead of trains through the Coquihalla Pass to look for slides or washouts.

Daily foot patrols checked the line, and brakes were tested before every down grade. McCullough, on foot, annually inspected every bridge and tunnel.

The first finished section of line to be built connected Brookmere (originally named Otter Summit) with Merritt on the CPR main line. When government inspector Orde looked at this work in September, 1911, he pronounced it "the best section of railway he had ever examined." In June, 1912, locomotive 131 was borrowed from the CPR, and flatcars equipped with hastily constructed wooden benches were hooked up to it so that a crowd of Merritt people could ride up to picnic at Glen Walker. (Glen Walker was named after E. G. Walker, a local ranch owner, while Nearby Kingsvale was given the name of another local rancher, Del King.)

McCullough and Warren wanted the KVR in operation by the end of 1915. In October of that year there remained only five miles of unfinished line in the Coquihalla Valley. Heavy fall rains caused a rockslide which completely destroyed the camp at Ladner Creek. Fortunately it happened at mid-day when the camp was empty, but it caused a delay in track-laying while the camp was re-located. The five-mile gap might still have been finished if the rain had not turned to heavy snow. Two snowplows were sent in, but at Coquihalla Summit ten feet of snow had fallen by the beginning of December and the plow crews were fighting not to keep the line open for construction, but simply to escape alive. One plow, being pushed by two locomotives in tandem, became derailed just west of Coquihalla and before it could be rerailed the train was trapped by additional snow. After the second plow was sent to the rescue, a massive avalanche came thundering down, covering the track with fifty feet of snow and trapping thirty-five work cars and all of the workers between Coquihalla and Ladner Creek. And on

December 24 another storm struck. The water in the locomotives froze. On December 27, 1915, McCullough conceded the contest and ordered all the men out. Three months later, when he snowshoed into the pass, he found the snow still thirty to forty feet deep in many places, several snowsheds reduced to kindling wood, and the bridge at Boston Bar Creek destroyed. There had been a phenomenal sixty-seven feet of snow at Coquihalla Summit that winter. The Coquihalla was a mean enemy.

On July 31, 1916, against all odds, the KVR was finished and daily passenger service was available from Vancouver to Nelson. Trains departed from Vancouver in the early evening, enabling the passengers to dine in style. Walter Dexter, who worked as a waiter on the train, remembered that "we still had silver service. The main meal would be on a silver platter which was placed in front of the dinner plate, and each vegetable was served in individual silver dishes.... We gave a complete service right down to finger bowls, if anybody wanted them." Clare McAllister remembered that "it was pretty classy in the Kettle Valley's pullmans, not to mention its diners. The ice tinkled in the tall glasses, the napkins of starched linen were folded in fancy shapes, there were oyster crackers which might miss plopping into the soup bowls if one did not aim carefully, as we swayed round tunnels and through snowsheds. I admired the waiters' spiralling arms, as they balanced their trays with a dexterity more incredible than that of ship's waiters in high seas." The train was usually composed of a baggage car, a first class coach, a diner, several day coaches and a sleeper. The train would reach Penticton the next morning and Nelson by evening. Leaving Nelson early in the day, it arrived back in Vancouver the following morning.

In September, 1916, Shaughnessy arrived in his brass-railed private car and the three great men of the KVR—

Shaughnessy, McCulloch, and Warren—made a special inspection tour. They sat on the open platform at the back of Shaughnessy's car, three very proud and happy men. The click of the tracks or the sudden clattering of the trestles accompanied their talk, as they watched the scenery slide by. The Kootenay-to-the-Coast railway had been built and southern interior B.C. trade was flowing down to Vancouver. Against all odds, they had done it. They had made the dream come true.

3

From Hope to Brodie

Exploring the 500 kilometres of the KVR, walking it in springtime when the cottonwoods are fragrant, sharing it with a black-berrying bear in August, watching a shower of golden aspen leaves blow across it in autumn, skiing it in winter, can become a life-time passion. To help railway enthusiasts find the railway line, the next four chapters will describe the stations and some of the events associated with them.

HOPE

Little remains of the KVR facilities at Hope except a section house built about 1915, situated at the corner of Hope Street and Cariboo Avenue. At the back of this house is a bunkhouse in original condition. The Hope Museum has the JESSICA station sign. The GN station, conspicuous as you enter Hope, is now being restored as a Community Centre. The KVR bridge over the Fraser River was built with an upper deck for moter vehicles, and a lower deck for trains. The upper deck is still used by vehicles leaving Hope to drive up the Fraser Canyon highway, but few drivers are aware of the section below, where the rails have been removed but the ties remain. It may be examined by walking in from Wardle Street.

OTHELLO & THE QUINTETTE TUNNELS

The first KVR station east of Hope is Othello, the site of the Quintette tunnels. This section of the railway is now an official park, under the supervision of The Hope & District Chamber of Commerce. There are, in fact, only four tunnels, but one was "daylighted" with large openings on the north side, giving the impression of a fifth tunnel. You can enter the tunnels from either the north or south end. To reach them from the north end, leave Hope on the Kawkawa Lake road, which becomes the Othello Road, and proceed east about four miles. There is a prominent Quintette Tunnels sign at the point where the Othello Road becomes part of the old KVR right-of-way. Park here and walk, as there is very limited room for parking or turning when you reach the tunnels. The Coquihalla River, hurrying to plunge into the narrow canyon, dances along on the left. Ahead gapes the black opening of the first tunnel. The Canyon is a narrow gap slashed through granite rock, its walls rising vertically from the river to a

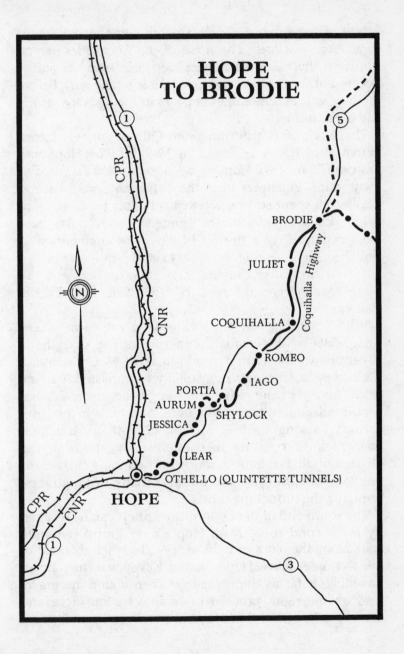

HOPE
TO BRODIE

1

5

BRODIE

JULIET

CPR

CNR

COQUIHALLA

Coquihalla Highway

ROMEO

IAGO

PORTIA

AURUM

SHYLOCK

JESSICA

LEAR

OTHELLO (QUINTETTE TUNNELS)

HOPE

CPR

CNR

1

3

height of more than 300 feet, smooth and almost without vegetation or ledges. The noise of the river fades as you step into the blackness. Dripping water splashes softly. Because of the curve of the tunnel, it is totally dark before the tiny spot of white light appears in the distance, at the end of the tunnel.

The work of transforming the Othello tunnels into a tourist attraction was begun in 1985 by The Hope and District Chamber of Commerce, using a Canada Employment grant. Engineers from the Canadian Forces Base at Chilliwack spent several weekends building a suspension bridge between two of the tunnels, but this has now been replaced by a timber bridge. The engineers also replaced the decking on the existing railway bridge between two other tunnels. The huge timbers and the steel spans were donated by the Canadian Pacific Railway.

While standing on the bridges between the sheer rock walls, with the foam and roar of the Coquihalla River below, the visitor should imagine McCulloch and his survey instruments in a small woven basket hanging from the top of the cliff. Other engineers had said that a railroad couldn't be built here. Working in his precarious rocking basket, McCulloch cut small ledges on which to rest his instruments. By choosing the alignment that required four short tunnels instead of one long one, he gave the builders many drilling faces, reducing the tunnelling time.

The south end of the Quintette Tunnels can be reached by the second route from Hope, a delightful two-mile walk along the old KVR right of way. To reach this end of the KVR line, leave Hope on the Kawkawa Lake Road, travelling as far as the cemetery. Then taking the gravel road on the right, proceed to an intersection of several gravel roads, one of them the old KVR line. There is room here to park a car. About a half-mile before reaching the tunnels, a sign marks the 1876 Hudson's Bay Company brigade trail. One can still hike along this section of a trail which became part of the famous Dewdney Trail. It runs into the huge gravel pit on the south side of the Othello Road. For a day's round-trip hike, walk through the tunnels from the north end and along the old railway grade to the Dewdney Trail, then climb over the hill to the gravel pit and from there go down the Othello Road to the starting point.

Leaving the Quintette Tunnels, Tunnel Road (Othello Road) runs north-east along the KVR right-of-way to join the new Coquihalla highway via an underpass. Just before the underpass, some CPR-red buildings may be seen behind a house; these are KVR buildings from Othello. The KVR grade (Tunnel Road) disappears under the new highway at this point. On the highway shoulder, a small oval sign (with a railway engine logo) announces OTHELLO. On the east side of the highway, an information sign points to the Hudson's Bay Company Brigade Trail plainly visible high on the steep slope of Mount Jarvis, the same trail as the one which crossed the KVR line west of the Quintette Tunnels. This trail ran from Hope east to Tulameen. The KVR, however, reaches Tulameen by an easier grade, going north to cross the mountain through the Otter Creek Valley.

LEAR

Driving north on the Coquihalla Highway, the oval sign marking LEAR is almost five kilometres from the Othello Road. The KVR grade reappears on the west slope as it climbs beside the highway. The site of Lear is now buried under the highway grade.

JESSICA

Nothing remains of this station site either, about seven kilometres north of Lear, near the point where the Jessica Bridge crosses the Sowaqua Creek. At the Sowaqua Creek picnic area, on the west side of the Coquihalla Highway, when the Coquihalla River is low, it is possible to wade the river and find the KVR right-of-way hidden in the forest.

AURUM

Approximately six kilometres from the Jessica Bridge, an oval sign marks the site of the flagstop first named Verona (another Shakespearian link) and only called Aurum when it served a gold mine. Here the highway crosses the Ladner Creek Bridge and in the distance, to the west, the railway bridge can be seen. Where Ladner Creek cuts a chasm across the railway route, a nine-plate girder span was built, 560 feet across. Near this bridge a camp was destroyed by an avalanche in 1915. This bridge can be reached by a steep climb through the Carolin Mine property, accessible from the Dewdney Creek turnoff. Coastal forest covers the valley slopes on both sides, with many broadleaf maples among the evergreens, and black cottonwoods along the river. In summer there are bluebells, Indian paintbrush, mimulas and daisies. In October the vine maples and blueberry bushes flame scarlet and gold.

SHYLOCK

Only two kilometres past Aurum, another oval sign announces the flagstop name Shylock.

PORTIA

North of Shylock about two kilometres, an oval sign indicates Portia Station. The railway grade looped north into Boston Bar Creek then crossed the creek at the present Portia Bridge. Here the highway swings west up the Boston Bar Creek Valley. Highway construction has removed any evidence of this part of the KVR, except a cement trestle foundation at the edge of the creek, underneath Portia Bridge.

At this point those in search of the KVR will leave the new highway, turning east at Boston Bar Creek on the old Coquihalla Road (which we will call the Coquihalla Pass Road), and follow the KVR route along the Coquihalla River. This gravel road rejoins the highway at the summit, at the Coquihalla Lakes. As the Coquihalla Pass Road leaves the site of Portia, it follows the route of the railway but the character of the area has been much altered by gravel quarrying for highway construction. Two kilometres from the Portia turnoff, the Coquihalla Pass Road turns sharply downhill, abandoning the railway grade. At this point it is possible to drive on the railway line for almost a kilometre to a gravel area, where the route has been blocked by bulldozing. For hikers this part is easily crossed and the railway grade continues northwards.

Approximately four kilometres further, the Coquihalla Pass Road again runs on KVR right-of-way, and soon the site of Iago may be found.

IAGO

Evidence of this station is now hard to find. A path leads to a rocky bluff overhanging the river far below. Here are cement foundation blocks and a tuscan red freight building. A short distance north there are two concrete pads on the west side of the right-of-way and the wreckage of a building. A path leads up the slope, following the course of a stream. There is a dam, and in the pool an intake pipe (6" wire-wound wood pipe) in a box with a mesh screen cover. Iago had both a water and a coal tower.

Trains coming down to Hope always stopped at Iago to

cool their brakes. It was just south of Iago that the runaway train of 1926 began to accelerate, going faster and
faster until it leapt from the tracks at Jessica. In 1917, a
fierce early December storm caused a snow and rock slide
which hit the rear of a plow train working near Iago. The
caboose tumbled 700 feet down into the canyon, killing
one man and injuring two others. McCullough was also
hurt in the slide, but walked twenty-five miles to Hope
on his damaged leg. Before that fall of snow had been
cleared away, another storm dumped more snow. It was
so deep that a two-engine plow train working south from
Coquihalla station was stalled in a drift near Romeo. At
the same time, a snowslide came down behind the plow
train, sweeping out part of the trestle at Bridalveil Creek,
leaving the part on which one end of the train was standing. The crew drained the locomotive and fought their way
out on foot. When there was a January thaw, the men
snowshoed back to the abandoned plow train and refired
the engines. Unfortunately the thaw also caused snow-
slides and it was almost three weeks before that train got
to Portia, thirteen miles down the line. The crew used
broken trestle timbers to fire the boiler.

The sectionman at Iago for the first twenty years of the
KVR operation was a man named James Porteous,
commonly known as "Coquihalla Red." Basing his pre-
dictions on the actions of a pair of eagles which nested in a
tree behind the sectionhouse, Red knew when slides
would occur. If the eagles flew along the railway, the line
would remain clear, but if they flew across the canyon,
Red would phone the dispatcher to get a crew, for within
an hour a slide would come down on the tracks. The
eagles' forecasting was too accurate to be merely co-
incidental.

If it was a snow slide, he'd call for the rotaries. According to KVR engineer Gordon Fulkerson, "I've seen lots of

time on those rotaries where we'd be pushing with three engines…we'd get a few feet, then we'd get a few more feet, and so on. And if we could get through, we'd just keep going right through, no matter what we tore off the end. We'd shut the cab windows or the snow would come in and fill the cab up, and we'd hold our hand up against them so it wouldn't come into the cab. It was a lot of fun.''

Engineer Fulkerson also had the unique experience of watching his own engine hit a rock slide on the Coquihalla. He was coming down from the Coquihalla summit with a double header (two locomotives at the front of the train) and it was thawing, so he knew that there was a danger of slides. Coming around a curve, he saw the tunnel entrance ahead blocked by a slide. "I goosed her and said to the boy: 'Jump!' I jumped. The snow was quite deep there and I went up to my knees. I just stood there fascinated. I said, "Here's once that I'm going to see one of these things go into one of them.'" The engine went right up on the slide. "We were quite a while cleaning that out. They had to detour the passenger trains around Spences Bridge...which they used to call 'going around the Horn.'"

In January of 1913, two miles beyond Iago, a sandcut had slipped down over the tracks, creating a slide 150 feet long and about 10 feet deep on the high side. KV railroad man F. Perley McPherson tells how they decided to try the rotary on it: "I said to the rotary engineer, a friend of mine and a great railroad man, 'Simon, did you ever fire this machine in sand?' He said, 'No, I never did.'...so we started and she worked like a charm, like a big concrete mixer throwing sand clear across the other side of the Coquihalla!"

About a kilometre and a half north of Iago, you will drive through a KVR snowshed. Dated 1944, it was built first of cement with later steel reinforcing and was constructed to replace a wooden snowshed destroyed by a snowslide. Not one of the fifteen wooden snowsheds of the Coquihalla section has survived. Two kilometres further the road passes through another tunnel, also dated 1944, with the inside reinforced with iron. North of this tunnel, where the road crosses a short railway bridge, a drilled drain-stack pierces the rock wall on the west side of the bridge. This was made by the KVR crews to lead a stream under the railroad. Frequently, spread along the mountain slopes, the bleached grey fragments of smashed wooden snowsheds lie scattered.

ROMEO

About eight kilometres north of Iago is the station called Romeo.

Perhaps one of the strangest stories of the KVR concerns a snowslide just below Romeo. Cliff Inster, a KV hogger (engineer) was working a helper engine. Cliff's engine was coupled to the front end of a coast-bound passenger train going down to Hope. Coming upon the snowslide, the engineers decided to cut their locomotives off the train and try to buck their way through. Cliff made a run at the drift. Stalled by the snow, he backed off and made a second run and was stalled again. Now the two engines in tandem roared at the drift, slamming it so hard they almost got through. But a headlight had been broken, so Cliff crawled over the engine's catwalk to inspect the damage and found himself staring straight down hundreds of feet to the canyon floor. A massive boulder had smashed the tracks and twisted them off the edge of the narrow ledge on which the railway ran. One more push would have sent the engines hurtling to disaster.

The statistics for Coquihalla are impressive: on average there is 469 inches of snow every winter, but the highest recorded fall for one year is an incredible 642 inches.

Now, driving the Coquihalla Pass Road beside the river, the KV route can be seen slicing along the mountain slope above, and soon it is also possible to catch glimpses of the Coquihalla Highway, high above the KVR. About nine kilometres from the point where the Canyon Road descended from the KVR, there is an iron bridge with the middle wooden section blasted out by modern engineers as an exercise. A kilometre to the north is magnificent Falls Lake

Creek trestle, which has iron truss girders with wooden trestle approaches. Behind it is the lovely Bridal Veil Falls, uncountable strands of shining water cascading over the rock face. In the winter of 1918, between Christmas and the New Year, low temperatures froze the falls into a veil of solid ice. Then a chinook blew down the valley and the ice toppled onto the bridge, knocking out four bents (supports).

North of the falls, the Coquihalla Pass Road climbs past three railway tunnels, reaching the KVR right-of-way at the end of the third, and from this point it is only two kilometres along the KVR right-of-way to the Coquihalla Lakes where an access road leads to the highway.

COQUIHALLA LAKES

A few pieces of broken cement may mark the site of the Coquihalla Station. Highway construction has removed any evidence of the water tower and the wye for turning the helper locomotives which assisted the freight trains up from Hope, some 3500 feet below. Now the railway has ascended to the sub-alpine lodgepole pine country. To the north, entering the dry interior, the ponderosa pine is conspicuous. The Indians from the Nicola Valley annually harvested the excellent blueberries and huckleberries of the Coquihalla Valley, but the best, they said, grew at the lakes.

Some say that the name Coquihalla is derived from Coqua-Halla, a Nicola Lake Indian with extraordinary powers. On either side of the Nicola Valley stand isolated pinnacles of dolomite, said to be the women collecting berries on one side of the valley and the men hunting on the other. These unfortunate people refused to come down to meet Coqua-Halla so he froze them into stone. Others assert that the name comes from the Halkomelem Kw'iykw'iya:la, meaning "stingy container" and referring to water pygmies who lived in river pools and tangled and teased the lines of fishermen.

At the Coquihalla Lakes an information sign describes how the Coquihalla Pass was used by the Nicola Valley ranchers to drive cattle down to Hope as early as 1875. Later miners and then loggers tramped this route. Here the railway ran from 1916 to 1959. In the 1960s the Trans

Mountain Oil Pipeline Co. ran its line along the abandoned railway. Then, West Coast Transmission brought its natural gas through the Coquihalla but avoided the upper Coquihalla Canyon by going via Boston Bar Creek, the route of the new highway.

About five kilometres further along the road (on KVR right-of-way) on the Coquihalla Lakes side of the highway, the road crosses the highway and turns north, passing over a KVR iron bridge. A short distance further to the north, the KVR reappears on the east side of the highway.

JULIET

About nine kilometres north along the highway, at a crossing of the Coldwater River, the oval sign for JULIET station appears. An access road turning to the east is a piece of the KVR line and crosses the river on a KVR iron bridge. The paved part of the railway/road goes to a picnic site. Near the iron bridge is an information sign describing the work of Chief Engineer Andrew McCulloch.

BRODIE

The site of Brodie station can be found by leaving the Coquihalla Highway at the Larsen Hill turnoff, about eleven kilometres north of Juliet. Alternatively, from Juliet you can go north on the KVR roadbed by driving under the highway at Juliet Creek, driving north beside the highway and going under it once more at Brodie Bridge. Brodie is at the southern bend of the "Big Loop", used by McCulloch to gain altitude. The point where the trackless grade of the Coquihalla section joins the tracked roadbed can be examined.

The fish stocks of the Coquihalla River, decimated by the rock slides of KVR construction, were further reduced when the oil and gas lines went through. In addition, forest

fires resulted in flash flooding of the river, which scoured
the spawning grounds. The silting of the river from the
Carolin Mines at Ladner Creek also discouraged the
salmon. In this once-great steelhead river, barely 200 fish
survived. Now, however, with the addition of hatchery
fish to the river, the run is recovering.

When McCulloch laid out the rail connection from
Merritt to Otter Summit (later named Brookmere) in 1910,
the route crossed and recrossed the Coldwater River to
avoid heavy rockwork and to maintain an easy grade.
Reaching the Otter River Valley, the railway turned back
on itself in the giant loop which enabled it to keep a steady
one percent grade through Pass Creek.

45

In 1913, fifteen dump cars being loaded with ballast broke loose at Brookmere and ran away down the grade towards Brodie. Locomotive engineer Jack Crosby, bringing a string of cars up the grade from Merritt, saw the runaway as it rocketed along the upper track of The Loop. Immediately he reversed his train. Skillfully he backed it downgrade at high speed until the runaway cars hit him with minimal impact. He was then able to slow down, bring the entire train under control and push the runaway cars back up the grade to Otter Summit.

To go from Brodie to Brookmere, you must return to the Coquihalla Highway by ascending the twisting gravel road up Larsen Hill. At the top of the hill there is an information sign about the Hope/Nicola cattle trail. Turn east off the highway at the Coldwater turnoff. A roadsign indicates the gravel road to Brookmere, sixteen kilometres away. At this turnoff an information sign gives a capsule history of the Kettle Valley Railway, calling it "a railroad like no other."

From Brookmere to Princeton

BROOKMERE

The village of Brookmere has a feeling of remoteness and peace, and the grass grows tall in the railway yard. The old store is closed. The artist Doug Strang sells his watercolour paintings in a small gallery near his house. One of his neighbours has a collection of rusting artifacts from Brookmere's boom years. Brookmere was the meeting point of the joint tracks, a divisional point for both the KVR and the VV & E (owned by the American GN).

In 1914, with both men and explosives being committed to the war effort, McCulloch and Warren were pressing the GN to finish the joint track between Princeton and Brookmere, which was graded but the tracks not yet laid. They wanted to complete the connection from the Kootenays to the coast (via Spences Bridge) lest the war completely shut down railway construction. The GN track-layers reached Brookmere on October 25, 1914. Louis Hill, acting for his father, drove a last spike, with an audience of GN officials who had come north over the new line in a special train from Spokane, and Merritt people brought in by a KVR train. The divisional point at Otter Summit was officially renamed Brookmere, honouring Harry Brook, a pioneer homesteader in the valley.

The GN built a round house, turntable and fueling tank. The railroads shared a water tank with both American and Canadian spouts, which still stands forlornly near the surviving KVR tracks. The station building was also placed squarely in the middle, the KVR tracks on the north side and the GN tracks on the south. The KVR also built a bunkhouse, coal tower, turntable and roundhouse, which have not survived. The GN station house is still there, now a private residence.

KVR engineer Gordon Fulkerson explained the role of the Brookmere coal tower in the delicate matter of keeping steam up in the locomotive boiler. The coal at Brookmere was Middlesboro coal from the Nicola Valley. It had been good at first, but "when they got back in a ways it was dirtied with slate and everything. I've seen them take a full tank of coal and when you're firing it all the time, you would be just picking the slate up and throwing it off the side, because it would build up in the firebox. Heck, in an hour you'd have the firebox full and you'd have to clean your fire again." The good coal came from Comox on Vancouver Island. The supply of coal taken on at Van-

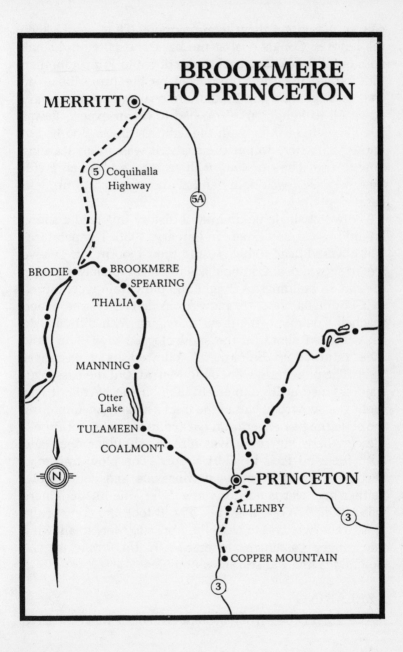

BROOKMERE TO PRINCETON

MERRITT

⑤ Coquihalla Highway

5A

BRODIE • • BROOKMERE

• SPEARING

THALIA

MANNING

Otter Lake

TULAMEEN

COALMONT

PRINCETON

ALLENBY

③

COPPER MOUNTAIN

③

N

couver would get them to Brookmere. They would keep the leftover Comox coal at the back and take on a small amount of Brookmere coal to run down to Princeton; then they would use the Comox coal on the Jura Hill up to Osprey Lake, and the Brookmere coal again for the easy downhill to Penticton. "You had to be an expert. It was just like going fishing with the light test lines. You had to know just where to put the coal...it was an art learning how to fire. The first two or three weeks I had an awful time because I was right-handed and you had to fire left-handed all the time."

The worst single tie-up in KVR history involved a snowbound train at Brookmere in January, 1935. Temperatures had hovered near 40 below, and then a storm hit. Twelve feet of snow fell at Coquihalla Station, completely covering the station buildings. A freight and plow train were buried in Coquihalla Pass. A plow train left Brookmere and reached Coalmont, the crew managing with difficulty to get it turned about on the snow-clogged wye. The plow then returned to Brookmere, followed by a passenger train. The plow train went on to Merritt, but the passenger train stopped at Brookmere to take on fuel. While it was fueling, a snowslide closed the tracks ahead. Encountering the slide, the passenger train backed to the safety of Brookmere, where the snow was already shoulder deep and both fuel and food in short supply. The plow train had become trapped in snow at Kingsvale and could move neither backwards nor forwards. Everyone in Brookmere was rationed to one meal per day. It took the crew of the plow train two days to clear the tracks to Merritt, allowing the hungry passengers to escape by that route, as the Coquihalla line was still snow-bound.

SPEARING

The gravel road from Brookmere south makes a large

loop eastward, away from the KVR tracks, bypassing the site of Spearing and rejoining the railway at the site of Thalia. Spearing was first named Koyle, which was confused with Coyle station near Merritt, so Koyle was renamed Spearing, after Gus Spearing who was an Otter River trapper. Nothing remains to mark this station.

THALIA

Driving east out of Brookmere, the road to Thalia turns north, crossing the KVR tracks. About sixteen kilometres of meandering road brings the traveller to the Otter Valley Road. Turning south the road winds nine kilometres past small ranches and through forest until it passes under the railway. This is the site of Thalia, but nothing remains of the station. Thalia had three name changes in its history: it was first named Canyon by the GN railway builders, after Canyon House, the first Otter Valley settlement. The KVR renamed it Roberts, after an Aspen Grove homesteader. Then both railways agreed to call the station Thalia, after a daughter of a GN official.

Thalia was the site of another runaway accident. In July, 1920, a freight train left Penticton headed west with ten carloads of fruit. At Princeton five cars of cows were added. Climbing up the Tulameen, the locomotive had malfunctioned, so the crew took it into the roundhouse at Brookmere. After repairs had been made, the engine was attached again to the train. But somehow the coupling that was three freight cars back had been broken. Suddenly the crew saw twelve cars vanishing down the 1.2 percent grade towards Princeton. The three remaining freight cars were quickly shunted to a siding and the locomotive set off in pursuit. The engineer dared not go too fast for fear of coming suddenly upon wrecked cars blocking the tracks. Ahead of them, the freely-rolling cars accelerated, careening wildly as the animals milled about in panic. A mile and a half west of Thalia the five cattle cars left the tracks, taking two fruit cars with them. All the animals were killed. The caboose and five freight cars kept on rolling, finally slowing to a stop at Otter Lake, 36 kilometres from Brookmere.

MANNING

Manning was named after the pioneer William Manning. It is located approximately sixteen kilometres south of Thalia, down the Otter Valley Road. A row of CPR freight cars, parked on a double-railed section of the railway, mark this station site.

Vancouver Public Library photo 36965

TULAMEEN

Ice for every ice-house west of Spokane was once cut at Otter Lake and packed into boxcars at Tulameen. The ice cutting operation usually began in late January and lasted about two weeks. In 1919, the record year for ice shipments, 3,000 boxcars of ice were loaded and shipped out in fifteen days. Several hundred men and many teams of horses were required for this work. The long ice trains rumbled continuously through Princeton. The invention of artificial ice put an end to this annual harvest and in 1925 the last ice train rolled south from Tulameen. The KVR used Osprey Lake ice for its refrigerator cars, for packing Okanagan fruit.

Ice was an insignificant product of the Tulameen Valley compared to coal. The coal mines of the Nicola Valley, first opened in 1907, had supplied locomotive coal to the CPR until 1912, when the CPR changed to the use of oil. In 1917, when the war caused an oil shortage, the CPR reconverted to coal. The coal from the Tulameen Valley was a lignite, used primarily for home heating. The KVR did not use this coal in its locomotives because it tended to cause bush fires along the line. J. J. Hill was not concerned with the incendiary danger associated with this coal. The day the VV & E reached Coalmont in 1912 he signed a contract for 500 tons of coal per day for the GN's many fireboxes. Nine coal companies operated in the Princeton area between 1909 and 1935, with five mines having railway spurs. Some of these spur lines may still be found.

Tulameen was first called Capement des Femmes, because Indian families were left here when the men were hunting or making war. Gold-seekers called it Otter Flats. In 1901 the townsite was surveyed. The big wooden hotels of Tulameen's boom days have not survived, but on Strathcona Avenue the KVR station now functions as a private house. The name Tulameen, an Indian word meaning "red earth", refers to the red ochre cliffs found along the river.

COALMONT

The village of Coalmont, eight kilometres south of Tulameen, boasts a number of false-front buildings from a bygone era, as well as the pretentious Coalmont Hotel. Perhaps the town would have died anyway, when the railways converted to oil, but the process was hastened by a terrible explosion in the Blakeburn mine (formerly the Columbia Coal & Coke Company) in August, 1930. The explosion blew out the portal of the tunnel, sealing the mine with hundreds of tons of rock.

Within minutes of the explosion, off-shift miners were digging frantically into this rock. The Chief Inspector of Mines was brought to the site on a "power speeder" which was standing by at Hope to rush him along the KV rails. One imagines the Inspector, perhaps wrapped in a blanket, and two railway men pumping the speeder all the way up the long grade from Hope and then down the Otter Valley. But, tragically, rescue efforts proved futile and forty-eight miners were entombed in the mine. The mine was re-opened, functioned briefly, then closed down forever. Coalmont slowly declined to the quiet village you can explore today.

A good road climbs nine kilometres up the steep mountain to the site of the Blakeburn mine, where the shafts are now plugged. The coal used to be carried by tramline south around the curve of the mountain, and then by an aerial line down the steep slope to the Coalmont station of the railway. The tramline roadbed and some of the aerial tramline towers still remain.

PRINCETON

In front of the Princeton Museum stands a CPR caboose. It is now being used as a tourist information centre, with the original pot-bellied stove and coal box intact, and the single bunk serving for pamphlet display. In 1910 and 1911, railway construction caused a building boom in Princeton. It was not the CPR but Jim Hill's VV & E which was the first railway to arrive and by 1909 he had built a station, water tank, and two-stall engine house. The VV & E station was turned over to the KVR in 1921 and was used until its closure in 1975.

When negotiations with the GN (VV & E) were over, it was agreed that the KVR would join the GN track outside of Princeton. Arthur Stiffe, who worked on a track-laying gang putting the rails into Princeton from the east, remembered that "we got to Princeton on the 29th or 30th of April...we were all standing there that day. I guess the boss was so happy about reaching Princeton that he didn't mind us not doing anything for a little while. The Great Northern train was due, the mixed train, from Oroville, Washington. I could hardly wait to see this thing. We heard this bloomin' beautiful whistle—and he came around—showing off, just a belting you know. These old work trains would go about 15 or 20 miles an hour—but he must have been going 40 or 45. But we had our joint in perfectly and he didn't have to slow down—but went barrelling right through, dust flying, waves his hat, blew the whistle, three or four times and stopped at the station. Everybody was excited seeing this train, going that fast and it was all shining—all polished up and painted."

South of the closed and boarded Princeton station building, there is a large loop of track that enabled the trains to turn, as well as a railway tunnel, though which one can glimpse the beginning of the Otter Valley.

ALLENBY, COPPER MOUNTAIN

South of Princeton rises Copper Mountain, whose copper ore was first claimed by "Volcanic" Brown in 1888. Brown said his Sunset mine would enable him to resolve all the world's problems by giving away money, but he later sold out for $45,000. The claim changed hands twice more before the Canada Copper Company began work in 1914. Wartime demand for copper spurred development and in 1917 the KVR agreed to build the much-needed spur line. To get the 2.2 percent grade required more than 30 trestles and 4 tunnels. Large amounts of solid rock had to be blasted from the mountain side to form a ledge for three hundred feet of track above the Similkameen River. About eighteen kilometres from Princeton, there is a half mile stretch of line that has four tunnels totalling 900 feet. But no sooner was the line finished in the autumn of 1920 than it was closed—the drastic drop in copper prices after the war forced the company to shut down the mine and concentrator mill. The next owners, the Granby Consolidated Mining and Smelting Company established a subsidiary, Allenby Copper, in 1923 but this enterprise was also soon closed down. In 1925 both mine and railway began operations again, with Granby running the mine. Production climbed to 2,000 tons per day, requiring a fifteen car ore train making three round trips per day from mine to mill. The concentrates were then taken to the Consolidated smelter at Trail, a healthy volume of work for the KVR.

The route of this branch line is difficult to follow by road, but can be touched at the site of Allenby, south of Princeton. Allenby was named for Field Marshall Viscount Allenby, a First World War general, and it was the site of the copper concentrator. The extensive open-pit operation at Copper Mountain has erased the original Copper Mountain mine and station. Southeast of Princeton, the Similkameen River railway bridge may be found.

From Princeton the Kettle Valley Railway climbs the mountain to the east, accompanied by the Hayes Creek Road.

From Princeton to Penticton

Tracks and ties are still in place along this section, but there is a path beside the rails for walkers.

BELFORT, JURA, ERRIS, JELLICOE

From Princeton, the rails of the KVR meander back and forth across the grassy hills to the east, giving the impression that they don't know or care where they are going. In fact, they are gaining altitude on a steady 2.2 percent grade. The paved highway we drove in pursuit of them crossed and recrossed the gleaming steel. No buildings remain to identify the station sites. Belfort was named after a French garrison in the Jura Mountains which rise on the Swiss border of France. Jura station had a water tank and wye for turning helper engines, at the point where the 2.2 percent grade slackened. Erris was given the name of an Irish Mountain, while Jellicoe, first named Usk, was renamed in 1916 to honour the British admiral of the Battle of Jutland.

OSPREY LAKE

At the summit of the Thompson Plateau, the divide between the Okanagan and Similkameen Valleys, the railway passes the three connected lakes named Chain, Link and Osprey. Osprey Lake was the source of ice for the KVR. The station was located at the east end of the lake, where there is now a large level field which serves as an emergency landing strip. The remains of the station may be found by noting a bus converted to a house above the road. At this point a path leads down to a wide meadow, with the railway track running along its edge. The station site is marked by a water tower base and the station building foundation. A wind sock bobs in the field.

THIRSK

At a crossing of Trout Creek, near km 27 on the road, is Thirsk Siding Forest Service Recreation Site. If you take the road to the north after crossing the bridge, you will

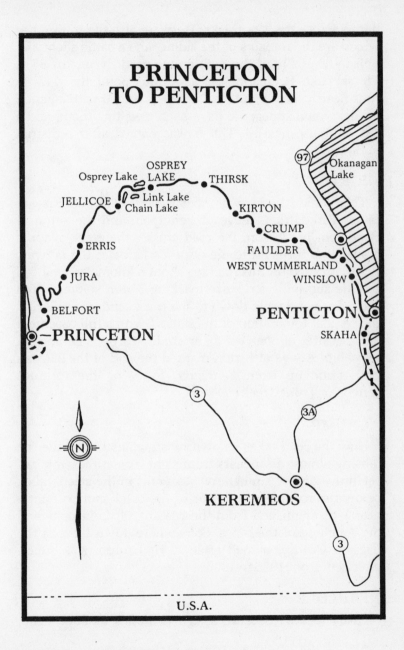

PRINCETON TO PENTICTON

OSPREY LAKE

Osprey Lake

THIRSK

JELLICOE

Link Lake

Chain Lake

KIRTON

ERRIS

CRUMP

FAULDER

JURA

WEST SUMMERLAND

WINSLOW

BELFORT

97

Okanagan Lake

PENTICTON

PRINCETON

SKAHA

N

3

3A

KEREMEOS

3

U.S.A.

bump across the KVR tracks. Here are also the rotting ties which are the remains of the siding, and a cattle shoot and pen indicates how the siding was used. Near km 34 is Thirsk Lake Recreation Area. At this point the railway runs nearby, above the road. There is a shed with a bench inside, which appears to have been a waiting room, and a red outhouse nearby. Thirsk was named after a district in England.

KIRTON

This station name was constructed from the Kir—of James Kirkpatrick, reeve of Penticton, and the —ton of Penticton. Just before the road crosses the creek again, a gravel road turns off to the north and crosses the railway. If you proceed on this road for about a kilometre, you can see the surviving structure marking Kirton station, a red shed. Park and walk down to the tracks and you will find the cement foundation of the station, with a full basement and a scatter of charcoal all around. Nearby is an ancient log cabin. A wye at Kirton marked the end of the 2.2 percent grade up from Penticton, following the tortuous canyon of Trout Creek.

CRUMP

Now the road takes its own twisting descent, while the railway almost disappears from sight. Sometimes you can catch the glint of sunlight on steel rails in the steep valley below the road. The murmur of the creek can be faintly heard, distinguished from the rustling of the aspens and the soughing of the pines. Somewhere down there is the flagstop Crump, named after T. H. Crump, KVR superintendent from 1925 to 1935.

FAULDER

Easily located because a sign identifies Faulder Road,

this station boasts a surviving station house as well as a freight shed and outhouse. Inside the station house is a supply of dry wood, an airtight heater, an iron cot, table and chair. Nothing more. Here new shiny rails run parallel to overgrown rails. This station was named after E. R. Faulder, a settler from 1891.

WEST SUMMERLAND

Now the road descends in rough gravel switchbacks into the Okanagan Valley. On this section of road watch for thundering logging trucks with their entourage of dust demons.

The station at West Summerland was for some time a most attractive museum, but it has now unfortunately been destroyed. The KVR almost missed West Summerland completely. The obstacle was Trout Creek. The route by-passing the gaping chasm cut by Trout Creek also by-passed West Summerland, and Reeve Ritchie and the townsfolk of West Summerland made such an uproar that a public hearing was held. The reasonable arguments did not appease them—they were determined to have the KVR pass through their town. McCulloch and Warren finally decided to alter the route even though it meant building the highest bridge on the entire KVR. The 400 feet of trestle-work for the approach to the steel span required so much timber that a new sawmill was built just to cut bridge timbers.

Murdoch McKay, McCulloch's assistant, has told how McCulloch argued with the Canada Foundry engineer, insisting that certain calculations for the Trout Creek bridge were wrong. Three KVR assistant engineers supported the Canada Foundry figures. McCulloch, with young McKay assisting, resurveyed the entire canyon, climbing up and down the canyon walls a dozen times one afternoon. Although McKay was a young man and Mc-

Culloch nearly fifty, McKay had a hard time matching McCulloch's pace, and at the end of the day McKay fell into his cot, exhausted. The next morning, he discovered that McCulloch had stayed up the entire night, working on his measurements and calculations. McCulloch subsequently overruled the Canada Foundry plan. Four months later, McCulloch, McKay and four other engineers watched as the final section of the 250 foot bridge was being placed...one quarter inch short of being a perfect fit! Appropriately, the KVR is called "McCulloch's Wonder."

The best view of the bridge is from the Agricultural Research Station at Summerland, accessible from Highway 97 near Sunoka Beach. A chain-link fence guards the edge of the breathtaking canyon, the metal span like a tight-rope across it.

There is an excellent new museum at Summerland that houses a large collection of KVR artifacts. Quite a few of them have been loaned by Jack Petley of Okanagan Falls, a leading KVR enthusiast, and there are many photos from Bill Presley. This is a place where railway buffs will linger, for there is much to examine. Summerland Museum, 9521 Wharton Street, is open during July and August only, from one to four o'clock, Tuesday to Saturday, and one to five p.m. on Sunday.

WINSLOW

On each side of the south end of Okanagan Lake, there are high glacial terraces, or benches, whose edges make an abrupt drop to lake level. These towering clay cliffs are prone to slumping and erosion when they are cut. As a result, the KVR was brought down to Penticton on the route formed by Shingle Creek.

PENTICTON

Penticton was selected for the KVR headquarters, and complete repair and servicing facilities were built. In exchange the city gave the KVR a section of lakeshore property for a depot. The first necessity was a dock, so that railway steel could be unloaded from the CPR boats running on Okanagan Lake. Concerned with getting the job done, McCulloch had his crew driving the first piling shortly after sunrise, without waiting for Reeve Foley-Bennett to give the event his official blessing. Awakened only minutes before the work commenced, the reeve came hurrying down to the dock, unshaven and fastening his suspenders as he ran, intending to perform some version of a sod-turning ceremony.

A few years later, in October, 1912, the town celebrated the arrival of the first locomotive. It was a gala occasion, and when locomotive KVR 3 had a good head of steam, Mrs. Warren had the honour of blowing the whistle loud and long. After her, many other Penticton citizens did likewise — a noisy, jubilant affair. An even more impressive celebration was staged in 1915 when the line was finished from Merritt through to Midway. The first passenger trains came from both east and west, bringing citizens from all over southern British Columbia, and more than half of Penticton's citizens were there to welcome them. The town band played, all the flags which could be found were fluttering, and bunting was draped on the Incola Hotel. Because of the numerous stops en route, the trains were late and no doubt the patient Penticton people drank many a toast during the long hours of waiting. At 4:30 p.m. the train from the east chuffed in and everyone cheered, but the train from the west didn't arrive until 10:15. The banquet at the Incola Hotel finally got started at 11 p.m. At 4 a.m., when the after-dinner speakers were still droning on, the electric light plant broke down. The last speeches were illuminated by the uncertain flicker of matches.

The Penticton station, built in 1941, is no longer in use. Pieces of the KVR right-of-way are now footpaths cutting diagonally across the city squares. McCulloch lived in Penticton, and here he died in December, 1945. He was buried in Fairview Cemetery on the slopes above the lake between Penticton and Naramata, in a grave overlooking the railway which is his monument. In 1959 the city erected a memorial to him in Gyro Park. There is a KVR exhibit at the Penticton Museum which includes railway jacks and a finger bowl.

OSOYOOS SPUR

The pressures of the First World War delayed construction of a branch line south from Penticton to Osoyoos, for the purpose of transporting fruit. After the war, an added incentive came in 1919 with the announcement by Premier John Oliver of a major irrigation and land settlement plan for the South Okanagan. The boggy nature of part of the valley made the line surprisingly expensive. In 1920 construction started on the two mile line from Penticton to Skaha Lake. There was to be a barge service down the lake, to connect with a line from Okanagan Falls southward, which was approved for operation in 1923. This spur line carried mainly fruit and a small amount of lumber. There was never a formal passenger service, but people were allowed to ride in the caboose. By the time a rail link had replaced the barge service, a good road and motor cars had made passenger service unnecessary.

A short distance west of the now boarded-up station on Hastings Avenue in Penticton, the railway line forks. The road to Princeton heads north up Railway Street and the spur line to Osoyoos bends south over the Okanagan River. It runs past what is now the Penticton Airport, and then along the edge of Skaha Lake. Down the line at Oliver the station is now the headquarters for the International Bicycling and Hiking Society, where the construction of the Okanagan Hiking Trail along the railway has already been started.

In Penticton, at the corner of Main and Preston streets is a sign: "The Okanagan Valley International Peace Park will some day pass near here. A portion of the route is now under construction. It is hoped that the entire 300 kilometres, from Brewster, Washington to Vernon, B.C. will be completed by Canada Day in the year 2000." The signboard in Penticton was dedicated by Rick Hansen, when his Man In Motion World Tour was in Penticton on May 13, 1987. As you read the sign, you can look down the KVR right-of-way, running through Penticton.

From Penticton to Midway

Now the KVR has climbed over two mountain ranges, over Otter Summit (at Brookmere) and Osprey Lake Summit. But it was the third plateau, the Okanagan Highland, which gave McCulloch the toughest challenges of his work. He spent a month examining the problem of how to bring the railway from the Hydraulic Lake Summit down 3,000 feet to Penticton. He wanted a 1.9 percent grade, but this required that the railway run around the outside of the mountain ridge, sixty tortuous miles requiring many tunnels and bridges. The alternative was to go through the Chute Lake Pass. As Chute Lake was at the same height as the Hydraulic Lakes, this route forced the line to descend 3,000 feet in only fifteen miles, an impossible 4.5 percent grade. McCulloch's solution was ingenious. He took the railway up a 2.2 percent grade from Penticton then doubled it back in a five mile loop (still keeping the 2.2 percent grade), and then doubled it back again through a long tunnel exiting just below Chute Lake. This is the longest stretch of 2.2 percent grade in Canada. There is easy access to this part of the line from a number of roads climbing the mountain on the Naramata side of Okanagan Lake.

ARAWANA

Leaving Penticton, going towards Naramata, the trackless rail line crosses the Lower Bench Road near Vancouver Place. Further along the Lower Bench Road, a sign points to Lakeview Cemetery, below which the KVR runs. From the cemetery northward, the orchards have been laid out across the KVR right-of-way, so that it only survives in short pieces. It crosses the Naramata Road at Poplar Grove Road, where large boulders block vehicle access. The station of Arawana, near Arawana Creek, is east of Naramata. The name of Arawana was taken from a song popular before the First World War, "Aeeah Wanna". Several roads, turning east up the mountain slope, give access to the railway line for walkers, but local people are in the habit of taking their cars up Smethurst Road (just

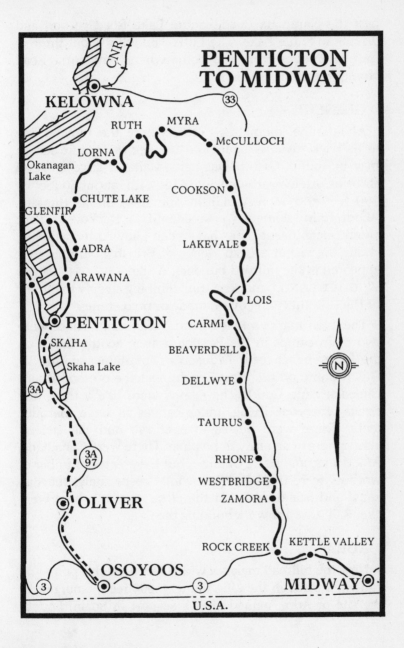

past the Naramata Road—Shute Lake Road corner) and driving to Shute Lake. The Little Tunnel is about three to four kilometres from the point where Smethurst Road crosses the KVR.

GLENFIR

About nine kilometres north, where the railway line turns back towards Penticton, the site of Glenfir station may be found. Glenfir was named after a large grove of fir trees. An overgrown square rock fill, about 50 feet by 100 feet and 15 feet high at one side, marks the site. About four kilometres past Glenfir is Rockovens Park where magnificent pines have been allowed to grow old, giving the visitor an experience of British Columbia as it appeared to the railroad builders. A sign, "RO.OS PARK. NO WOOD CUTTING," marks a trail climbing steeply to the site of the sole surviving oven, made of field stones.

The oven marks a KVR construction camp. There were two main camps in the Penticton area: Scott's Camp on the lower bench near Munson's Mountain and the Big Gulch Camp on the West Bench, near the present Mount Chapaka Auto Court. The camps were like a three-ring circus, everyone living under canvas in large marquee tents. There were horses in a corral, and the general atmosphere of an army in bivouac. There were Canadians, Americans, and some Chinese, but the greatest number of workers were from Europe, from Greece, Italy, the Balkans, and Scandinavia. At the close of 1912, there were over 2,000 men at work building the KVR.

ADRA

Now the railroad makes a wide U-turn. At this point you can walk through the long tunnel (1604 feet), emerging at the site of Adra, named after a seaport in Spain. Foundations of a station and water tower remain to mark the site, about one kilometre north of Adra Tunnel. Both Arawana and Adra had water tanks and there were extra tanks at Mile 86.8 and Mile 96.7, anticipating much huffing and puffing up the long 2.2 percent grade.

NOTE: It is possible to bypass the tunnel, *which appears unsafe*, by climbing the road through Rockovens Park. The views of Okanagan Lake are splendid.

CHUTE LAKE

From Naramata a good road climbs to the Chute Lake Resort, passing a few feet from the site of Glenfir Station. The resort, on the site of Chute Lake station, is a large log building, with a spacious dining room in which the owner, Gary Reed, has hung many photographs of trains and trestles. He is making good use of several red KVR buildings, and a picnic table stands on the octagonal cement base for the vanished water tower. There was also a wye at Chute Lake.

LORNA

Leaving the resort, you can drive east along the KVR line to Lorna, but this is now an active logging road and caution is advised. Approximately 15 kilometres from Chute Lake, an opening in the trees gives a first view of Kelowna. Another 7 kilometres further east there is an abandoned trestle, where a rock cut and fill have replaced the old route. About 24 kilometres east of Chute Lake, the station of Lorna can easily be missed. A stone foundation overgrown with alder is on the south side of the line. An outhouse is hidden behind the station foundation. Two kilometres east of Lorna is the curved steel bridge over Belleview Creek, the altitude of 4014 feet marked on the cement foundation.

For anyone who might consider climbing one of these trestles, the story of Hector Richmond's ascent is a cautionary tale. In 1923, Richmond, accompanied by another student, was sent to the site of the Lorna trestle to study the bark beetle. Perhaps bored by the solitude, he decided to climb the twelve-tiered trestle, each being about 15 feet in height and braced diagonally with timbers bolted to upright stanchions. Descending to the bottom of the ravine, Richmond started to climb. He went up easily enough to start with, but when he was half-way up, he looked down and, according to his report, his hair stood on end. He tried to retreat but found that descending was even more difficult and dangerous than ascending, so he continued upwards. When he reached the top, exhausted and fearful, he discovered that the deck of the trestle extended three feet beyond the upright stanchions. Panic-stricken, he realized that he would have to reach out and get a grip on the squared timber rim, hang perilously in space and then haul his body up and over the edge. "At last I was lying on top of the trestle. I was a nervous wreck, too shaken to stand, scarcely able to speak."

RUTH

This station was first called Kelowna Siding but was renamed Ruth, after Andrew McCulloch's daughter. Seven kilometres beyond the Belleview Creek trestle, the Little White Forest Service Road (from Kelowna) crosses the right-of-way. East of this crossing, a rock slide blocks the line for vehicle access to Myra Canyon, the most exciting nine miles of the Kettle Valley Railway. Hikers can continue along the right-of-way but vehicles must descend to Kelowna on the logging roads (**safe on weekends only**).

MYRA

This next station is on the eastern end of Myra Canyon, accessible from Kelowna by two alternative routes. The first, by way of McCulloch Road from East Kelowna, is an active logging road; unless you wish to travel in fear of the giant trucks descending in clouds of dust, this road should be used only weekends. The alternative is longer: follow Highway 33 east out of Kelowna and drive about 39 km until you turn west on McCulloch Road. When you turn into the McCulloch Lake Resort, you will cross the KV line. Driving west on the railway right-of-way you will come, within one kilometre, to the causeway across the end of the lake and the site of the station named after Andrew McCulloch. If you continue west along McCulloch Road, past the Wardlaw farm at the end of the lake, you can turn south to rejoin the KVR line and drive to Myra Canyon.

At the site of Myra station there is a wide clearing and the foundations of the station building. A short distance westward the line enters the breathtaking Myra Canyon. Even the imperturbable McCulloch was startled by his first view of this mammoth gash in the mountain. "Never saw a railway built on any such hillside as this," was the comment he penned in his journal. "Villainously heavy" construction would be required, he added.

Myra Canyon *is* spectacular! Far away below, 3000 feet down, Kelowna lies in its nest of mountains. At first, walking across the trestles with the mountain falling away below your feet can be unnerving. There are safety platforms, two boards wide, jutting over space, formerly used to escape an approaching train. When the forest fires threatened these trestles, crews, choking in the thick smoke, the sweat pouring from their smudged faces, sprayed water on the trestles to save them.

In an article in the Okanagan Historical Society magazine, David Wilkie lists the specifications of the Myra
Canyon bridges, tunnels and trestles, Mile 84 to 89.5:

MILEAGE		BENTS	LENGTH & DEPTH IN FEET
84.	Myra		
85.	Trestle	13	180 x 31
85.20	Trestle	7	90 x 26
85.25	Trestle	7	90 x 39
85.30	Trestle	11	150 x 40
85.35	Trestle	17	240 x 38
85.45	Trestle	20	285 x 48
85.60	Trestle	7	90 x 32
85.65	Tunnel		375 feet
85.90	Trestle	30	434 x 80
86.35	Tunnel		277.5 feet
86.40	Trestle	14	193.8 x 31
86.50	Steel bridge		365 x 158
86.55	Trestle	17	240 x 70
87.40	Trestle	21	295.5 x 81 (S curve)
87.90	Steel bridge		721 x 182
88.00	Trestle	6	75 x 10
88.20	Trestle	35	495 x 122
88.40	Trestle	19	270 x 30
88.60	Trestle	32	465 x 86
89.40	Trestle	25	360 x 49

The steel bridge at 86.50 consists of five spans, crossing
the East Fork of Canyon Creek, while the steel bridge at
87.90 has twelve spans over the West Fork of Canyon
Creek.

This section of the KVR, featured in the 1973 film "The
Canadian Dream," is unrivalled in the world as an
example of railway construction of the early twentieth
century.

Vancouver Public Library photo 1771

Walter Dexter, a waiter on the KVR, remembered that "the train travelled very slowly on some stretches, particularly over the wooden trestles. I can remember vividly how those trestles creaked as the train went over them, probably going no more than five miles an hour.... Some of those trestles curved around a gorge and sometimes when looking out the window it appeared that there was nothing under the train, and a very long drop. It was a bit frightening and eerie."

In July, 1923, at West Fork Canyon Creek, a freight car derailed on the giant wooden trestle and fell into the canyon, dragging several cars with it. Far below, in the smashed wreckage of the cars, lay eight cases of dynamite bound for the Highland Bell mine at Beaverdell. If one of those cases had exploded, the 180 foot high trestle would have collapsed, severing the KVR.

The trestles are in good condition, renewed with treated timber in the not-too-distant past. Only bridge 88.4 has untreated timber; the base of this bridge has timber cribbing filled with rock.

McCULLOCH

Returning from your exploration of the canyon, McCulloch station, at the west end of the causeway, is marked by a Tuscan red freight shed with many of the boards torn off. To the west, just where the farm fence blocks further travel on the rail line, the cement foundation of the water tower may be found. The water came down to the water tank from a small lake to the north.

COOKSON

From McCulloch the line curves to the south. Washouts block the line but hikers and bicyclers can cross them easily. The next station, Cookson, may be identified by the red freight shed or tool shed. Cookson was named after a pioneer rancher at Kallis Lake.

LAKEVALE

Lakevale was first named Arlington, and to reach this station by car it is necessary to drive east on McCulloch Road to Highway 33, then south about 18 kilometres. A sign marks the road to Arlington Lakes, climbing three uphill, rough and rocky kilometres west to the railway right-of-way. At the south end of the southern-most of the Arlington Lakes is a Forestry camp site, used infrequently by fishermen, and this is also the site of Lakevale station. The large cement foundation for the water tower is above the Tuscan red pump house, at the lake's edge. The night we camped there, the loons were courting at dusk and their strange laughter echoed across the lake.

LOIS

A rockslide prevents all but the hardiest of four wheel vehicles from driving from Lakevale to Lois, so it is necessary to return once more to Highway 33. Fifteen kilometres to the south, turn west on Wilkinson Road and climb back up to the KV line and follow it north-wards, high above the West Kettle Valley. The red freight shed survives, its door creaking as it swings in the mountain wind. Lois, a flagstop, may have been named after the daughter of a tracklaying foreman. From Hydraulic Lake to Carmi, the railway has an easy one percent grade.

CARMI

It is only a few kilometres south to the village of Carmi, connected to the rail line by way of the Carmi Station Road. Now, it is almost a ghost town, but in 1914, when the railway was being built, Carmi had a gold mine, a jail, a hospital, two hotels, two stores and gas stations. Now, greying buildings have sagging rooflines. A hotel is boarded up. At the station site there is the foundation for the station house and two red sheds behind. Nearby rise huge mill buildings. In 1896 an American, Jim Dale, staked the Carmi mine, naming it after his Illinois hometown. Five years later he sold it to a British group which immediately received a contract to deliver 1500 tons of ore to the Boundary Falls smelter, which meant hauling the ore by wagon fifty miles to Midway. The Phoenix paper remarked hopefully that "a railroad will quicken the entire country wonderfully and make many mines out of present prospects." At Carmi, a ten-stamp mill was built, but in 1914 the mine was sold to a new syndicate, which was attracted by the fact that the KVR passed right through the property. The old workings were cleaned out and the mill enlarged. In 1920 there was another change of ownership and by 1939 the Carmi mine was finished. The village's brief life was essentially over, and its inhabitants drifted away.

BEAVERDELL

The Highland Bell silver mine, 2500 feet above Beaverdell on Wallace Mountain, has been in continuous operation since 1900. An eight mile road from Beaverdell climbs almost to the summit of Wallace Mountain; a twenty minute walk leads to a viewpoint with a magnificent hundred-mile view in every direction. It's like being on the crest of a huge wave in a sea of mountains. The lively village of Beaverdell has an old hotel (claimed to be the oldest B.C. hotel still in use), and outside stands a KVR railway signal in a bed of petunias. The mill buildings beside the rail line are still functioning to process ore, now transported by trucks.

DELLWYE

Continuing south of Beaverdell on Highway 33 and turning west on the Tuzo-Eugene Forest Road, after crossing the West Kettle River, you again meet the KVR line, at the site of Dellwye station. All remains of the station were probably bulldozed away when the forestry road was constructed. From this point it is possible to drive the KV line south to Taurus station.

TAURUS

This station was originally named Bull Creek, but as the name was already in use for a place near Fort Steele, it was renamed Taurus. There are foundations for the water tower and the station, and a red shed behind the station site. When we were there in July a trail led down from the shed through a froth of daisies to a ford across the West Kettle River. Proceeding southward the rail line enters a dramatic river canyon after crossing the river on a bridge that has a few missing ties. You can also reach this canyon by returning to Highway 33 and driving south a few kilometres. The trail access to the Bull Creek Canyon section of the KVR is not easy to find. It is about one kilometre north of the point where the north end of the Blythe-Rhone road rejoins Highway 33, about 300 yards north of a sharp corner where a rock cliff shows blasting. The debris from this work blocks the rail line below. Bull Creek Canyon is a narrow rock pass where the west fork of the Kettle River doubles back on itself. Using a number of tight curves, the KVR line squeezes through without tunnelling.

RHONE

Turn west off Highway 33 on the Blythe-Rhone Road, which crosses the river then turns onto the KVR grade. The site of the station (named after the French river) is somewhere among the few scattered houses and small farms which constitute the village of Rhone. The Blythe-Rhone Road recrosses the river and brings you back to Highway 33. To the south is an excellent country store and post office named Westbridge.

WESTBRIDGE

You can buy gas as well as groceries at the Westbridge store. The site of the KVR station is on the south side of the highway bridge, identified by the cement foundations of the railway building and fragments of burned, red wooden siding. The grade of the railway follows the curve of the river.

ZAMORA

South from Westbridge on Highway 33, a road named Zamora Road turns east towards the river. A cluster of houses probably identifies the site of the station. Continuing south on Highway 33, you can catch glimpses of the KVR sometimes curving with the river and other times taking a straight line across the flood plane, occasionally dissolving into the blowing grass of some farmer's hayfield.

ROCK CREEK

About seven kilometres south of Zamora is Provincial Camp Site No. 134, on the Kettle River. The KVR right-of-way passes through this park then crosses the Kettle River on a twinspan Howe truss bridge. There is good swimming in the shallow, swift-flowing river and the camp site is delightfully shaded from the summer heat.

Rock Creek village, two or three kilometres south, was the site of the short-lived 1860 gold rush. When the first KVR train from Vancouver rolled into Rock Creek, it was greeted by a cheering crowd and the storekeeper, Tom Bansen, presented the engineer with a gorgeous wreath of roses to be hung on the engine. At Rock Creek, the abandoned KVR line now runs through the centre of the village, disguised as a road, and passes the dolomite plant. Going north out of the village, the KVR road can be driven for a mile or so along the bank of the river, then, at a point where the KVR becomes grassy trail, the gravel road turns right, up the hill, and the railway right-of-way becomes part of a farmer's field.

KETTLE VALLEY

The Kettle River was so named because of huge whirl-pools in the shape of pots or kettles, to be found far downstream from the Kettle Valley community. The small cluster of houses which is the present Kettle Valley village is located where a one-lane bridge crosses the river, but there is no sign of a station.

MIDWAY

Midway is supposedly halfway across British Columbia. The original townsite was plotted in 1893. It is at the junction of three wagon roads: the first headed west to the Okanagan, the second ran north, and the third went south to the Colville Reserve. The C & W railway reached Midway in 1899, and in 1905 the VV & E (GN) connected Midway with Spokane.

It was in Midway in the fall of 1905 that the long contest between the CPR and J. J. Hill's Great Northern erupted into the Battle of Midway. This was a struggle between two hastily assembled armies of railway construction workers, fought mainly with clanging shovels and work-hardened fists. Fortunately, no one was killed. The trouble began when the GN crew began cutting a tunnel through a rocky hill at Myers Creek, about seven miles west of Midway, crossing a piece of CPR line — lot number 2703. CPR workmen erected barricades and posted guards on the CPR lot, determined to make things as difficult as possible for the GN. On November 7, 1905, GN men attacked the barricades with picks and shovels, pushing into the CPR camp and knocking down tents. Outnumbered ten to one, the CPR men fled. A telegraphed message brought reinforcements and the CPR men returned to establish a strong camp on their own land, from which they sallied forth to rip up and carry off GN track. The GN put guards along their right-of-way and chained their tracks to anchors drilled into bedrock. They brought in a carload of barbed wire from Spokane. The CPR men continued to rip up track. The opposing armies were both camped on the disputed strip of land, only 25 feet from one another.

The weather was cold and grey. Both sides were keeping warm with liquor from the United States, only a mile or two south of Midway. Tempers mounted and suddenly the two "armies" rushed at each other, fists and picks swinging. At this point the provincial police arrived on the scene, and the "war" was moved to the courtroom. The CPR obtained an injunction ordering the GN men off lot 2703, but the GN commenced expropriation proceedings and on December 8, 1905, the British Columbia Supreme Court awarded ownership of lot 2703 to the Great Northern Railway. The GN won the battle, but was destined ultimately to lose the war. The road to the site of this angry fracas runs south out of Midway,

Vancouver Public Library photo 9851 — wreck

Wreck of a CPR ore train at Phoenix, near Grand Forks. This photograph was taken around the turn of the century.

crosses the river, and turns west to the dump. This is, in fact, the GN railway grade. West about nine kilometres, at a point where the road turns abruptly uphill, abandoning the railway grade, is the site of the Battle of Midway, nearby on private property. The road climbs uphill to avoid the five tunnels of the GN railway.

Midway Station is to be reopened as a museum. The railroad station was, for each district, the focus of the whole area — the place of departures and arrivals, of tears and laughter, where packages and telegrams arrived, where the clicking telegraph key seemed to have a life of its own and where train orders were handed up to the engineer looking down from his window in the hissing locomotive.

The grade of the ill-fated Midway & Vernon Railway, begun in 1901 and abandoned in 1905, begins about a mile and a half west of Midway station. At the time of construction it continued nearly to Rock Creek (9.5 miles). In 1905 the CPR extended its trackage 2.5 miles west of Midway station paralleling the M & V grade. In 1910, the KVR simply graded a connecting section from the end of the CPR track to the M & V grade and used the M & V line into Rock Creek as its roadbed. Railway buffs may wish to identify the mile of original M & V grade still visible 100 feet north of the CPR track, starting at the entrance roadway of the sawmill.

In the village of Midway, two blocks south of Highway 3, a small museum has a CPR caboose, and a section of track with a small car to run on it. The Museum is open May 17 to September 15, 10 a.m. to 4 p.m. daily. Where Highway 3 crosses the Kettle River between Kettle Valley and Midway, the KV right-of-way passes beneath the highway bridge; here the line is a walking trail along the river's edge, through the fields. The narrow green valley curves between the high mountain walls, with the placid river sliding gently down toward the U.S. border.

The Kettle Valley Railway ends at Midway, but of course it was always part of the Canadian Pacific Railway system, so the rails run on, out of Midway, towards the Rockies and through the Crowsnest Pass to Alberta and the East.

The Decline
of the Kettle Valley Railway

In 1929, when the CPR main line was closed by a train wreck, the KVR carried all the East-West freight and passengers. Recognizing the value of this bypass, the CPR was willing to bear the cost of maintainance and improvement, and a number of bridges and trestles were replaced. Some were built of steel, as if the railway were to last forever. In 1930, the CPR formally took over the operations of the KVR, now officially named the Kettle Valley Division of the CPR. In the Kootenays, it was still called the KV.

Andrew McCulloch retired in 1933, aged 69, after 23 years with his railway; he lived to reach his 81st birthday. He travelled in the U.S. and Europe but preferred hunting and fishing in the country around Penticton. He had always thought that British Columbia was the best place in the world, and the Okanagan the best of British Columbia. He especially enjoyed hiking with J. J. Warren along sections of the railway. In 1937 Warren wrote to McCulloch from North Carolina:

Dear Chief;

I had a nice letter from you in December. There isn't anything you say appreciative of the years we were together that I won't agree with. In fact they were in many respects the happiest days of my life and you were the main factor in that happiness. It is not often that men of mature age become such friends as we did — and are. Those journeys together and the unexpected occurrences will never be forgotten and unfortunately cannot be repeated.... Then we used to speculate as to what in H--- would be carried by the railway, and now see the loads go by....

The number of loads was destined to decrease. The slow decline began after the 1930 takeover. Adding to the world-wide economic depression, the summer of 1931 was so hot and dry that the fruit crop was a disaster. This was a significant loss of revenue for the KVR as well as for the farmers. At the same time a plague of grasshoppers filled the air, many dying on the railway right-of-way. According to Barrie Sanford, they "so severely greased the rails that the few trains which were running could hardly move." In July a forest fire near Portia almost burned a score of railway bridges and in August a forest fire burned a section of line near Carmi. This was the year the crews heroically saved the trestles of Myra Canyon.

As the depression continued, unprofitable rail lines were abandoned elsewhere in Canada. Snow was a major problem for the KVR from the beginning, but 1935 was the year of the worst single tie-up in KVR history, when twelve feet of fresh snow covered the railway buildings at Coquihalla summit. This was the year when the passenger train was trapped at Brookmere with insufficient food. The same winter the temperature went from below zero to 50 degrees Fahrenheit and a released ice jam swept down the Tulameen and badly damaged the Howe-truss railway bridge five miles west of Princeton.

When forest fires in 1938 burned three major wooden trestles near Romeo, the CPR announced the abandonment of the Coquihalla section. They then changed their minds and rebuilt the trestles. The Second World War's increased demands for ore, coal and lumber kept the KV freight cars rolling. Four years after the end of the war, the Hope-Princeton highway was opened. Air travel and the automobile took the railway's passengers and the trucks took much of the freight business. The closing of Granby smelter at Copper Mountain ended 20 years of ore-hauling. In November of 1959 there were four separate washouts, all severe, but it was not until January of 1961 that the CPR announced the closing of the Coquihalla Pass section. As if to underline the firmness of their decision, the tracks were removed. At Brodie, on the afternoon of October 24th, 1962, a small group of railroaders, almost all life-time employees of the KVR, gathered to watch the last spike pulled up. The man performing this ceremony had seen, forty-six years earlier, the last spike driven home in Coquihalla Pass, when he and the KVR were young. Now he pulled the last spike and stood silent. Asked to give a speech, he could find no words.

They were proud men, those railroad men. Many of them had an unassuming self-confidence that came from learning a job and doing it well, a job that required self-reliance and judgement and courage, a job on which other peoples' lives depended, a job that pitted them against danger and discomfort. A good fireman could keep up the steam in a locomotive. A good engineer could control a heavy freight on a long downhill, knew all the danger spots, could start a train so smoothly that the sleepers in their berths slept on.

On a clear, crisp winter's day, January 17, 1964, there was one last publicly-advertised run from Spences Bridge to Penticton. Kathleen Dewdney was one of the passengers: "I remembered the daily passenger trains with crowded cars, especially during the war years; the diner with its immaculate linen, shining silverware, and delicious meals; the friendly porter who greeted us and prepared the comfortable pullman berths; and the freedom and relaxation of train travel."

Another traveller, Clair McAllister, recalled that "The trains left a trail of cinders and steam behind, but within we were kept immaculate by the porter's polishing brush and whiskbroom. We leaned against plumped pillows of goosedown, watching the snowy dusk blacken into night, until only our own reflections showed from black windows. Once it was our greatest need in B.C., our dream come true, our movement of wealth, our way of travel.... And they've run the last train through on the Kettle Valley Line....They've killed the Kettle Valley Line."

Did the CPR kill the Kettle Valley Line? In June, 1987, in the British Columbia Legislature, Jim Hewitt, the Member for Boundary-Similkameen, asked two questions: "First, are the branch lines uneconomical, or do the railway companies make them that way? Secondly, what happens to the railway right-of-way when the line is abandoned?" Hewitt read a letter from the mayor of Midway, asserting that the CPR had reduced service and allowed the line to deteriorate, in order to apply to the Canadian Transport Commission for abandonment. Chris D'Arcy, the Member for Rossland-Trail echoed this opinion: "The CPR's action over the last 30 years has been to deliberately set the stage for abandonment of all of their rail lines in the southern interior of British Columbia, and governments of this province...have stood by and let this happen."

The Hon. Jack Davis, Minister of Energy, Mines and Petroleum Resources, joined the discussion, giving his opinion that the rail lines in southern B.C. were no longer economically feasible. Concerning the question of abandonment, however, he stated: "the right-of-way should revert to the Crown provincial. It was gifted by the province to these railways initially on the under-standing — indeed, on the commitment — that they would provide transportation services." He also noted that the capital costs of the railways were eventually shouldered by the people of Canada, "in other words, were written off, and they are now operating without having to pay the interest on very large debts." The discussion ended with Mr. Hewitt's appeal for action: "Where the railway abandonment is allowed, the right-of-way should revert to the Crown."

If the KVR right-of-way reverts to the Crown, British Columbians must then determine its use. Of course, farmers will want to own the piece that cuts across their land, and the waterfront trackage will be in high demand.

But would it not be preferable, for the province and the world, to make this 500-kilometre long snake of right-of-way into The Kettle Valley Railway Historical Trail, one of the great hiking and biking trails of the world and a fitting monument to the age of steam railways?

The government of the United States has established a Rails to Trails Conservancy, to deal with the abandonment of more than 3000 miles of track each year. Already there are 85 rail trails and 60 or more currently in the development stage. The Director of the Conservancy programs, Peter Harnik, argues that the nearly level rail trails can be used by those incapable of climbing mountainous paths. Rail trails traverse every environment, urban to wilderness, often offering the hiker a fascinating variety of landscapes within short stretches of the route. Sometimes the rail corridors are prime wilderness conservation areas. They can be an important asset in areas woefully short of recreational opportunities. They have been shown to increase property values since many people wish to have a linear park in their neighbourhood. Also, the rail trails have been significant in local economies, with trail users spending money on food, camping, hotels, souvenirs and bicycle rentals. The fear of increased vandalism has proven groundless.

The International Bicycling and Hiking Society, with headquarters at Oliver (Box 5, Oliver, B.C., V0H 1T0) is working hard to make the KVR hiking trail a reality. Membership is $12.00 (single or family), $25.00 for Clubs. Communities along the route are invited to establish their own chapters of the I.B.H.S. The flood of letters to the Heritage Conservation Branch of the British Columbian government indicates a strong demand to save what remains of the Kettle Valley Railway. In the words of Stan Upton, Volunteer Co-ordinator of the I.B.H.S., we will be able to "peddle through Paradise!"

Epilogue

In May, 1989, the last train may have clattered over the sagging rails of the neglected Kettle Valley line. Perhaps the mournful whistle will never again echo down the mountain valleys. A public hearing process must follow the CPR's notice of intent to abandon the line, and tracks cannot be taken up until five years have elapsed. Now is the time for all hikers, bikers and railway buffs to save the right-of-way as a linear park. Please write letters to your government.

The Kettle Valley Ghost Train
by Arnold Jones

If you're driving east of Hope up Coquihalla way
Take heed of what I'm telling you and make the trip by day.
To drive by night is scary for there's no telling when
The Kettle Valley Ghost Train will fly those grades again.

You may call it superstition but I know this isn't so,
'And I know they tore her tracks up over thirty years ago)
But when men have built a railroad where a railroad shouldn't be
And have fought with mountain rock and snow through winter's misery,
And have dared to battle nature, and sometimes the men have won,
Their wounds and scars stay with them long after the job is done.
Long after their fears and curses, long after the blood and sweat,
They're haunted still by memories of struggles they can't forget.

They remember the daring blasting crews that worked on the steepest
   slopes,
How they drilled and shot their dynamite while tied to the rock with
   ropes;
And those men who died on the mountain side when the snows above
   let go
And swept the work trains, track and all, to the river gorge below.
But with tunnels, bridges, trestles and cuts they made those rails run true
And for every hundred feet of track the grade rose two-point-two.

Officials drove the last spike home and then they rode the line,
And though they praised the workmanship, pronouncing it as fine,
They scheduled trains with passengers to run the pass at night,
Lest timid souls aboard the cars should panic at the sight
Of canyons yawning far below, and chatter through their teeth
''This bloody railroad's built on air, with nothing underneath!''

And did they give the stations names like Shere or Thunder Ridge?
Or Avalanche, or Hanging Rock, Slide Creek or Windy Bridge?
They gave them names from Shakespeare (to calm all thoughts of fear)
Like Romeo and Juliet and Jessica and Lear.

The last spike had been driven but the battle still raged on,
For train and engine crews took up the battle, never won.
Against those Coast Range blizzards when winter still is king,
And it snows at the rate of a foot an hour and smothers everything,
And telegraph wires are buried, and slides maroon the trains
When the cuts that snowplows fought to clear are drifted shut again.

When the line was at last abandoned it wasn't the men who lost;
The decision was made by Brass Hats who had counted up the cost
Of fighting a losing battle with a foe that always won
In the economic warfare of freight rates charged per ton.

So they salvaged her rails and her bridges, and with scarcely a thought of
   respect
They demolished her snowsheds and trestles that men gave their lives to erect;
And all that remains to show that steam trains once had brought life and
   sound to these hills
Are the high mountain tunnels whose roofs bear the proof in the coal smoke
   that's showing there still.

It's in these mountain tunnels that the Ghost Train hides by day
Until another railroader is due to pass away.
It's then that the Ghost Train flies again and her whistle mouthes his
   name
In a way he's never heard before yet somehow sounds the same,
And her headlight shines upon him and it makes his eyes grow dim
And he hears her bell a-tolling and he knows it tolls for him.

It's the Kettle Valley legend: When a railroader gets old
And his legs can't reach the ladders and Life's boiler fires grow cold,
When his eyes can't read the orders and he's running out of steam —
That's when he sees the Ghost Train and he hears her whistle scream.

The Great Dispatcher's calling him and he knows the reason why:
He's now a one-way dead-head to that Terminal in the sky
Where there's never a wreck or washout, nor slide nor runaway
And he'll always win at poker and it's payday every day.

The red board's set against him and he's reached the end of track,
And at last he's got his miles in and he won't be heading back.

You may never see the Ghost Train but still you'd best beware;
Just because you cannot see her doesn't mean she isn't there.
That patch of fog on the road ahead that blocks your headlights' beam,
That fog may not be fog at all, but K.V. Ghost Train steam
So if you're driving east of Hope up Coquihalla way,
Remember what I've told you and be sure to drive by day;
To drive by night is scary for there's no telling when
The Kettle Valley Ghost Train will fly those grades again.

Maps

For excellent Ministry of Forests maps, write to:

Regional Recreation Officer, Ministry of Forests, 515 Columbia Street, Kamloops, B.C. V2C 2T7; 828-4131. Ask for the Penticton area, Princeton area, and Boundary District sheets.

Tourist Information Centres

Hope Travel Infocentre, 919 Water Avenue, Hope, B.C., V0X 1L0; phone 869-2021.

Merritt Travel Infocentre, Box 189, Merritt, B.C., V0K 2B0; phone 378-2281.

Princeton Travel Infocentre, Old Train Caboose, 167 Vermilion Avenue, Princeton, V0X 1W0; phone 295-7816.

Summerland Travel Infocentre, 7519 Prairie Valley Road, Box 1075, Summerland, V0H 1Z0; phone 494-2686.

Penticton Travel Infocentre, Jubilee Pavilion, 185 Lakeshore Drive, Penticton, V2A 1B7; phone 492-4103.

Midway History Museum, 6th Avenue & Haynes Street, Midway, V0H 1M0; 449-2413.

Campsites Along the KVR

Note: The following listings have been included to give you an idea of the range of campgrounds available. It is not meant to be a comprehensive listing, nor a recommendation of any facility.

HOPE

Camper's Roost Park, R.R. 3, Hope, B.C. V0X 1L0; phone 869-5007. North of Hope approximately 13 kilometres, this campsite features 52 sites, coined showers, laundry, shade, heated pool, store, etc.

Cariboo Trail Park, R.R. 3, Comp. 1, Hope, B.C. V0X 1L0; phone 869-9024. Approximately five kilometres north of Hope, this campsite features 30 sites, year round store, hot showers, short walk to Lake of Woods for swimming and fishing, shade, etc.

Coquihalla River Park, 800 Kawkawa Lake Road, Hope, B.C. V0X 1L0; 869-5671. Features 120 sites, coined showers, etc.

Hope Koa Kampground, R.R. 2, Hope, B.C. V0X 1L0; phone 869-9857. Approximately five kilometres west of Hope, this campsite features 150 sites, store, games room, heated pool, etc.

Hunterville Campsite, 59440 St. Elmo Road, Hope, B.C. V0X 1L0; phone 869-5132. Approximately 13 kilometres west of Hope, it features 30 sites, laundry, recreation room, free showers, shade, etc.

Nicolem River Provincial campsite: may be reached from Highway 3, a few kilometres east of Hope.

Othello Tunnels Campground, 67851 Othello Road, Hope, B.C. V0X 1L0; phone 869-9448. Approximately eight kilometres east of Hope, it is within walking distance to the tunnels. Features 30 sites, store, ice, showers, laundry, etc.

Poole's Evergreen Resort Campground, Kawkawa Lake Road, Hope, B.C. V0X 1L0; phone 860-9012.

Wild Rose Campground, R.R. 2, Hope, B.C., V0X 1L0; phone 869-9842. Approximately six kilometres west of Hope, it features 68 sites, store, laundry, hot showers, etc.

MERRITT

Claybanks Campground, 1300 Voght Street, Box 189, Merritt, B.C. V0K 2B0; 378-6441. Features 50 sites, showers, shade.

THALIA

Three kilometres east of Highway 5A are a cluster of ten Ministry of Forests campsites at Johnny Lake, Rickey Lake, Clifford Lake, Thalia Lake North, Thalia Lake South, Goose Lake North, Goose Lake South, Lokwick Lake South, Stoney Lake and Lodwick Lake North. These are small, treed sites with good fishing and some boat launching available.

TULAMEEN

Otter Lake Provincial Campsite is a large site with 45 spaces.

COALMONT

Cascade Wilderness Adventures Inc., General Delivery, Coalmont, B.C. V0X 1G0; phone 295-7632. Prairie platform tents, solar heated showers, privies.

Granite Creek Ministry of Forests Campsite is situated next to the Granite City Historical Reserve at the Junction of Granite Creek and the Tulameen River.

PRINCETON

Castle R.V. Park, R.R. 1, Site 1, Comp. 7, Princeton, B.C. V0X 1W0; phone 295-6250. This campsite is approximately eight kilometres east of Princeton, just past Sunflower Downs race course. It features hiking, horse corrals, showers, washrooms, etc.

Martin Lake Ministry of Forests Campsite is approximately three kilometres northeast of Princeton off the Hayes Creek Road.

JELLICOE TO OSPREY LAKE

Chain Lake, Link Lake and Osprey Lake all have small Ministry of Forests Campsites with minimal facilities, fishing and boat launching.

THIRSK TO WEST SUMMERLAND

There are four Ministry of Forests Campsites in this stretch: Thirsk Lake, Thirsk Siding, Demuth and Trout Creek Crossing. These sites are small and shady, with creek fishing.

SUMMERLAND

Balcarra Motel & Campground, P.O. Box 644, Summerland, B.C. V0H 1Z0; phone 494-4201. One block west off Highway 97, this site is near restaurants and shopping.

Cedar Brooke Campground, Highway 97, R.R. 2, Summerland, B.C. V0H 1Z0; phone 494-0911. This 44 site campground is near Sunoka Beach, and features free hot showers, laundry, heated pool, and shade.

Illahie Beach, Box 705, Penticton, B.C. V2A 6P1; phone 494-9800. This site features a private beach, boat launch, store, laundry, free showers, and tenting.

Lakeshore Tent & R.V. Park, 15419 North Lakeshore Drive, Summerland, B.C. V0H 1Z0; phone 494-8149. Shaded beach sites, boat launch, horseshoe pitch, 68 sites, coined showers, and camp store.

Peach Orchard Campsite, Box 159, Summerland, B.C., V0H 1Z0; phone 494-9649. Close to town centre, this site has 125 sites, tennis courts, coin showers, and shade.

PENTICTON

Banbury Green R.V. Park, Box 237, Penticton, B.C. V2A 6K3; 497-5221. Approximately six kilometres south of Penticton, off Highway 97. Lake frontage.

Camp-Along Tent & Trailer Park, Highway 97 South, Box 706, Penticton, B.C. V2A 6P1; 497-5584. South of Penticton five kilometres, opposite the game farm. Orchard setting, laundry, heated pool, store, showers.

Cherry Park Tent and Trailer Park, 3301 Skaha Lake Road, Penticton, B.C. V2S 6G6; 492-5811. Near the beach, park, and shopping.

Garden R.V. Park, 3310 Skaha Lake Road, Penticton, B.C., V2A 6G4; 493-7204. Adjacent to waterslides, public beach, and shopping centres.

Happy Hour Campground, R.R. 2, Site 40, Comp. 14, Penticton, B.C., V2A 6J7; 493-8506. On Highway 97 at the south entrance to Penticton. Arcade, mini golf, trampolines, snack bar, and store.

Lake Skaha Tent & Trailer Park, 3700 South Main Street, Penticton, B.C. V2A 5J8; 492-6322. East side of Skaha Lake, adjacent to public beach.

Pleasant Valley Campsite, 1701 Penticton Avenue, Penticton, B.C. V2A 2N6; 492-6988. Turn at Penticton Avenue off the Main Street. On Penticton Creek, this site features a par three golf course, and a snack shop.

Riverside R.V. Park, 271 Wylie Street, Penticton, B.C., V2A 5Y2; 492-0594. Shaded sites, free showers, laundry, near golf, shopping, and the beach.

Skaha Beachcomber Recreational Park, R.R. 2, Site 25, Comp. 9, Penticton, B.C. V2A 6J7; 492-8828. Shaded sites, laundry, store, propane, arcade, etc., opposite the beach.

South Beach Gardens, 3815 Skaha Lake Road, Penticton, B.C., V2A 6G8; 492-0628. Adjacent to Skaha Lake, with shaded sites, store, laundromat, arcade.

Waterworld R.V. Park, 185 Yorkton Avenue, Penticton, B.C., V2A 3V3. Adjacent to waterslide, with beach nearby. Has an arcade, mini golf, jacuzzi, pool table, store.

The Willows on Skaha Campground, 198 Skaha Place, Penticton, B.C. V2A 7L1; 492-3122. Adjacent to Skaha Lake, free showers.

Wright's Beach Campsite, R.R. 2, Site 40, Comp. 4, Penticton, B.C., V2A 6J7; 492-7120. On Skaha beach, with shade, etc.

CHUTE LAKE

Chute Lake Ministry of Forests campsite.

Chute Lake Resort, R.R. 1, Site 16, Box 16, Naramata, B.C., V0H 1N0; 493-3535. Rustic log cabins with wood stoves, or rooms in lodge. Restaurant, store, boat rentals, fishing, and tackle.

McCULLOCH LAKE (Hydraulic Lake)

Hydraulic Lake Ministry of Forests campsite has good lake access, boat launching, fishing.

McCulloch Lake Resort Ltd., Frost Road, R.R. 4, Site 21, Comp. 6, Kelowna, B.C., V1Y 7R3; 764-4852. Housekeeping cabins (bring bedding), wood stoves, boat rentals, store, ice, cross country skiing rentals.

McCulloch Ministry of Forests campsite borders on Hydraulic, Minnow and Haynes Lakes.

BEAVERDELL

Beaverdell Hotel, Box 40, Beaverdell, B.C., V0H 1A0; 484-5513. This is the oldest operating heritage hotel in B.C. Pub.

TAURUS

Two kilometres east of the highway at Taurus, there are three well-developed Ministry of Forests campsites at Taurus Lake.

ROCK CREEK

Two or three kilometres north of Rock Creek is the Kettle River provincial campsite. The railway right-of-way passes through this park and crosses the Kettle River on a truss bridge. A shady site with good river swimming.

MIDWAY

Zodiac Lodge, Box 36, Midway, B.C., V0H 1M0; 449-2662. Motel, with dining lounge and coffee shop. River and creek fishing nearby.

Bibliography

BOOKS

Burrows, Roger G. RAILWAY MILEPOSTS: BRITISH COLUMBIA. V.2: The Southern Routes from the Crowsnest to the Coquihalla. Vancouver, Railway Milepost Books, 1984.

Hope & District Historical Society. FORGING A NEW HOPE.

Richmond, Hector Allan. FOREVER GREEN. Lantzville, B.C. Oolichan Books, 1983.

Riegger, Hal. THE KETTLE VALLEY AND ITS RAILWAYS. Pacific Fast Mail, P. O. Box 57, Edmonds, WA 98020.

Sanford, Barrie. McCULLOCH'S WONDER. North Vancouver, B.C. Whitecap Books, 1981.

Turner, Robert D. RAILROADERS: RECOLLECTIONS FROM THE STEAM ERA IN B.C. Sound Heritage Series No. 31, Victoria, Provincial Archives of British Columbia.

ARTICLES

Belyk, Ralph: "The Midway Railway War," in CANADA WEST, November, 1986.

"The Coming of the Railroad," in Okanagan Historical Society, HISTORIC SOUVENIR OF PENTICTON, 1958.

Dewdney, Kathleen: "The Kettle Valley Railroad," in the Boundary Historical Society, FIFTH REPORT, 1967.

Donaldson, Bert: "History of Beaverdell and Carmi," in the Boundary Historical Society, SIXTH REPORT, 1971.

Douglas, Gilean: "Auto-less travellers can take trip to Wonderland," THE VANCOUVER SUN, August 15, 1953.

"Ghost Town Trails" (re Coalmont), in CANADA WEST, Fall, 1977.

Harnik, Peter: "Converting Abandoned Railroad Corridors to Trails," in 1st International Congress on Trail and River Recreation, 1986.

McCallister, Clare: "Death of a Railway," in BRITISH COLUMBIA HISTORICAL NEWS, February, 1972.

McCulloch, A.: "Railway development in southern British Columbia from 1890 on," in the Boundary Historical Society, FOURTH REPORT, 1964.

Macorquodale, Ruth: "Andrew McCulloch and the Kettle Valley Railway", in Okanagan Historical Society THIRTEENTH REPORT, 1950.

Shinnick, John: "On the K.V.R.," in OUTDOORS, April, 1983.

Sismey, Eric: "Kettle Valley field day," in THE DAILY COLONIST, May 30, 1971, page 10.

Trower, Peter: "No Hope," in VANCOUVER magazine, November, 1986.

Wilkie, David: "The Many Trestles of Myra Canyon," in the Okanagan Historical Society 43: pages 22-25, 1979.

Wright, R.: "Naramata Ovens," in B.C. MOTORIST, April, 1970.

Kettle Valley Railway Stations

	MILES	KILOMETRES
Hope	0	0
Othello	5.4	8.7
Lear	9.1	14.7
Jessica	14.5	23.4
Aurum	16.0	25.7
Portia	19.9	32.1
Iago	24.7	39.8
Romeo	30.2	48.6
Coquihalla	36.3	58.4
Juliet	44.5	71.6
Brodie	50.3	81.0
Brookmere	54.3	87.4
Spearing	58.0	93.4
Thalia	60.0	96.6
Manning	70.0	112.7
Tulameen	76.7	123.5
Coalmont	80.7	129.9
Princeton	92.5	148.9
Belfort	97.8	157.4
Jura	102.9	165.6
Erris	109.7	176.5
Jellicoe	117.3	188.8
Osprey Lake	124.5	200.4
Thirsk	130.6	210.2
Kirton	137.5	221.3
Crump	142.8	229.8
Faulder	147.5	237.4
West Summerland	153.5	247.0
Winslow	156.2	251.4
Penticton	163.0	262.3
Arawana	171.0	275.1
Glenfir	177.4	285.4

	MILES	**KILOMETRES**
Adra	183.5	295.3
Chute Lake	190.1	305.9
Lorna	198.9	320.0
Ruth	205.4	330.5
Myra	212.9	342.6
McCulloch	220.0	354.0
Cookson	226.4	364.3
Lakevale	235.5	378.9
Lois	242.5	390.2
Carmi	250.0	402.3
Beaverdell	254.1	408.9
Dellwye	257.2	413.8
Taurus	265.3	426.9
Rhone	271.9	437.5
Westbridge	276.2	444.4
Zamora	277.7	446.8
Rock Creek	285.4	459.2
Kettle Valley	287.8	463.1
Midway	296.7	477.4